The FinTech Ecosystem in the Czech Republic

OECD
BETTER POLICIES FOR BETTER LIVES

Please cite this publication as:
OECD (2022), *The FinTech Ecosystem in the Czech Republic*, OECD Publishing, Paris, https://doi.org/10.1787/068ba90e-en.

ISBN 978-92-64-63573-9 (print)
ISBN 978-92-64-57536-3 (pdf)
ISBN 978-92-64-80067-0 (HTML)
ISBN 978-92-64-68857-5 (epub)

Photo credits: Cover design based on: © kotomiti/Getty Images; Iaroslava Kaliuzhna/Getty Images.

Corrigenda to publications may be found on line at: www.oecd.org/about/publishing/corrigenda.htm.

Foreword

FinTech innovation has the potential to drive productivity gains, enhance economic growth, encourage innovation that spurs job creation and improves the quality and diversity of financial services. It can promote financial inclusion for the underserved or underbanked parts of the population, such as SMEs without collateral or prior credit history, or citizens in remote areas of the country. Data is at the core of FinTech financial applications. The provision of many such services is enabled by financial innovations where data usage is a cornerstone. Fostering FinTech innovation can strengthen competition in the market, while at the same time allowing the penetration of international markets.

The level of innovation and technical complexity of certain FinTech applications lead to a perceived uncertainty by the market about the existence and/or applicability of relevant regulatory/supervisory frameworks. Such uncertainty hinders the full exploitation of the benefits of financial innovation. This highlights the benefit of regulatory sandboxes for the entire ecosystem, including regulatory and supervisory authorities. In this regard, sandboxes and other innovation facilitator arrangements are critical as they allow small-scale testing of innovation in a controlled environment supervised by the competent authorities, assisting them to better understand the regulatory treatment of this testing phase, while also allowing engagement in a constructive dialogue with supervisory and regulatory authorities.

Against this backdrop, a technical support Project has been launched in May 2022, funded by the European Union via the Technical Support Instrument (TSI) and in cooperation with the European Commission's Directorate-General for Structural Reform Support (DG REFORM), together with the Organisation for Economic Co-operation and Development (OECD) as the designated implementing partner. The project falls in the area of administrative and regulatory reform, and seeks to unlock the potential of FinTech applications and the use of data in financial services in the Czech Republic and to examine the possible establishment of a sandbox in the country to enable FinTech innovation on the basis of data sharing and usage. The development of the FinTech sandbox features as a milestone of the Digital pillar of the Czech National Recovery and Resilience Plan (RRP), which is focused on digital technologies and aims at creating sandboxes in regulated sectors in line with EU priorities. Its successful completion will have a significant importance from political, economic and social perspectives, contributing to the top EU priorities – Green and Digital Transition.

This report provides an overview of the FinTech market in the Czech Republic (firms, activities, products and competitive environment, enabling environment and challenges) and the relevant local ecosystem in which it operates. The report also provides an overview of the current regulatory and supervisory frameworks relevant for FinTech in the country and an assessment of the potential impact of the new EU legislative proposals on this sector. The report also underlines the existing obstacles to FinTech development in the Czech Republic, including access to data, and relies on input provided by the Czech FinTechs through an online OECD survey, and to bilateral consultations with stakeholders involved in the Czech FinTech ecosystem.

Acknowledgements

This report is the outcome of a comprehensive consultative process that involved representatives from all different stakeholder groups of the Czech FinTech ecosystem, including financial supervisors and regulators; data-related authorities; incumbent market participants from different sectors of the financial markets; FinTech start-ups, SMEs and industry associations with a focus on FinTech activity.

The report has been prepared by Virginia Robano, Ana Sasi-Brodeski, Michala Stupkova, Hyojeong Kim and Iota Nassr under the supervision of Robert Patalano of the Division of Financial Markets of the OECD Directorate for Financial and Enterprise Affairs. Liv Gudmundson provided editorial and communication support.

The authors gratefully acknowledge the valuable input and constructive feedback provided by Lenka Frančе Rejzková and Alex Ivančo from the Ministry of Finance of the Czech Republic.

The report has been produced as part of the "Feasibility study on the potential of data in financial services" Project. It is financed by the European Union through the Technical Support Instrument (TSI) in co-operation with the European Commission's Directorate-General for Structural Reform Support (DG REFORM). The OECD is the designated implementing partner by the Commission for this Project.

For more on this Project, please visit https://www.oecd.org/finance/oecd-project-on-data-in-financial-services-in-the-czech-republic.htm.

Table of contents

FIGURES

TABLES

Executive summary

There were more than 100 FinTech companies operating in the Czech Republic when this report was prepared, active across a number of regulated and unregulated sectors of activity. The most represented areas in terms of number of companies are accounting, payments, savings and personal finance, P2P lending and investment crowdfunding. Many Czech FinTechs provide services similar to other globally successful FinTechs (e.g., "buy now, pay later") services. Czech FinTechs operate in a domestic financial services market which is heavily dominated by banks. Banking sector assets comprise 85% of the total assets of the domestic (regulated) financial system, while 64% of Czech citizens' assets lie in bank deposits (as of March 2022).

Financial market activity in the Czech Republic, including FinTech activity, is regulated by the Ministry of Finance of the Czech Republic (MFCR) which develops and enacts the financial market policy and drafts legislation. The Czech National Bank (CNB) is the sole unified supervisory authority for the financial markets in the ountry. It supervises the banking sector, capital markets, insurance and pension funds, financial intermediaries and distributors of financial products, payment service providers and non-bank consumer credit providers. In cooperation with the MFCR, the CNB participates in the preparation of primary legislation and is responsible for the preparation of secondary rules in the form of decrees and measures of a general nature. The CNB authorises, regulates, supervises and issues penalties for non-compliance with the financial market rules. Both the MFCR and CNB also promote financial education in the Czech Republic.

In its supervisory activities, the CNB applies a risk-based approach, allocating the largest proportion of its resources to areas that are systemically the most important or the riskiest. Traditionally, the CNB has refrained from acting as a supervisor for non-systemically important non-deposit taking institutions.

The CNB maintains its approach towards innovation in finance, which is a technology neutral supervision. The Czech Republic does not currently consider crypto-assets as money and instead classifies them as intangible assets. As such, providers of services in crypto assets are required to obtain a trading license from the Trade Licensing Office (within the Ministry of Industry and Trade) but are neither authorised nor supervised by the CNB or by any other supervisory authority.

In November 2019, the CNB established a FinTech contact point. The contact point aims at helping to resolve unclear regulatory issues – including licensing and supervisory ones – so as to facilitate compliance with the duties applied to market participants by financial market regulations. Opinions of the CNB provided via the contact point do not substitute for authorisations or approvals granted in licensing proceedings and are not binding in any way.

EU legislation proposals currently under way will bring more entities into the regulatory scope, to achieve a harmonised legal framework across the EU. This will ultimately increase the number of entities that the CNB will need to authorise and supervise. The objective of the EU, as it can be interpreted from recent initiatives such as the Digital Finance Strategy and the Open Finance consultation, is that FinTech growth should be actively supported and that access to data should be regarded as a major enabler of financial innovation.

Access to consumers' account data using Application Programming Interfaces (APIs) enabled on the basis of the Payment Services Directive 2 (PSD2) framework serves as an important source of data used by a significant part of the Czech FinTechs. The revision of PSD2 by the EU may thus have an important impact on the accessibility of third parties to users' financial data; while the proposed amendment to the electronic IDentification, Authentication and Trust Services (eIDAS) regulation could have an additional significant impact on the provision of financials services and would also have a direct effect on the industry-led Bank ID initiative.

In June 2022, the OECD launched an online open Questionnaire on FinTech activity in the Czech Republic. Twenty-four FinTech companies provided detailed responses to this Questionnaire as of 5 October 2022, representing almost a quarter of the total of c.100 Czech FinTech companies' universe.

Access to data is critical for FinTechs and data is at the core of most FinTech activity (e.g. artificial intelligence business models in trading; lending; blockchain-based solutions in finance). Indeed, more than 67% of respondents to the OECD Questionnaire stated that access to both financial and non-financial data is beneficial to their business development. Data collection, processing and analytics play a key role in FinTech innovations. Based on the responses to the Questionnaire, most FinTechs use data for the development of products and services and it is at the core of their business model. In particular, 88% of firms use APIs to access data, more than half of respondent firms use big data and 63% of firms use cloud computing.

When it comes to data sharing secured by formal regulatory arrangements and frameworks, such as PSD 2, data accessibility is not guaranteed. More than 46% of firms responding to the OECD Questionnaire have had problems accessing customer data from financial intermediaries.

Regulation of financial services safeguards market integrity, protects consumers and promotes financial stability. From the industry standpoint, it provides legal certainty that allows companies with innovative business models to develop and grow. At the same time, regulatory compliance is usually perceived by young start-up firms as a hurdle, given the associated cost and time commitment. According to the findings of the OECD Questionnaire, the most important reported hurdles to FinTech innovations in the Czech Republic are related to regulation: lack of regulatory clarity (67%), red tape (63%), licensing and supervisory requirements (58%), followed by entry barriers (54% of respondents). FinTech respondents signal as additional challenges the issues of access to market and business development.

Regulatory sandboxes are one of the policy tools being used in many countries to assist companies requiring authorisation in overcoming the challenges of market access, through the creation of an open dialogue between the regulator and the firm, they improve the supervisory and regulatory framework. Sandbox arrangements enable firms to test innovative financial products and services and ameliorate business models, subject to the specific rules applied by the supervisory authorities. Although sandboxes can involve the use of legally provided discretions by supervisory authorities, the baseline assumption for such sandboxes is that firms are required to comply with all relevant rules applicable to the activity they are undertaking. In terms of funding, empirical evidence suggests a beneficial impact of sandbox participation for fundraising of companies, facilitating access to finance which has been highlighted as one of the most important impediments to the establishment and growth of SMEs in the Czech Republic and beyond.

According to the OECD survey, 71% of respondent FinTechs would be interested in taking part in a sandbox with a focus on data, if it were to become available. Two-thirds of these would only be interested in participating depending on the terms of such a sandbox. A majority of respondents (77%) believe that a regulatory sandbox in the Czech Republic would also benefit the local FinTech sector and prefer that such a sandbox is focused on data. The answers highlight the importance of a well-thought design and structure of any future sandbox arrangement, and also a possible lack of clear understanding of what a sandbox involves from the FinTech side, underlining the importance of clear communication and the required educational effort that may need to be undertaken ahead of a possible future establishment of a sandbox.

Regulatory sandboxes can foster innovation in the financial sector while allowing supervisors to observe and address emerging risks of the deployment of innovative technologies in finance, with potential benefits that extend to all stakeholders involved. They may allow supervisors to enhance their understanding of innovative mechanisms deployed by FinTechs that may alter the risk profile of certain financial activities, which, in turn, may have a beneficial impact on the development of adequate policy responses to such innovations. Importantly, they may reduce regulatory uncertainty for FinTechs and may help lower the perceived regulatory burden for FinTechs in the Czech Republic that has been observed in the OECD survey.

1 The Czech FinTech market

There are more than one hundred regulated or unregulated FinTechs operating in the Czech Republic, mostly in areas such as accounting, payments, savings and personal finance, Peer-to-Peer and crowdfunding. Czech FinTechs operate in a market heavily dominated by banks. Czech traditional financial services providers are also active in the FinTech sector; they establish accelerators, operate venture capital funds and acquire equity of FinTechs. Banks are required to allow connectivity to view customer account data and to initiate payments under the Payment Services Directive 2, but FinTechs experience operational difficulties when connecting through the Application Programming Interfaces set up by banks. FinTechs often resort to aggregators to access data. There is a Czech Standard for Open banking, however it is not mandatory. Bank ID is a method of verification of identity built upon the connectivity framework which allows users to log in to the portals of companies and state administration.

Czech financial services are dominated by banks in most sectors of the financial market. The assets of the banking system as of March 2022 comprise 85% of the total assets of the domestic (regulated) financial system, including pension and investment funds, insurance companies and others (CNB, 2022[1]). 64% of the assets of Czech citizens lie in bank deposits (MFCR, 2021[2]). Banks are the only institutions allowed to directly operate in CERTIS, the central-bank operated Real Time Gross Settlement System for the Czech Koruna (for more in-depth description of the Czech financial sector see Annex A). Banks are the sole provider of mortgages to households although there is some non-bank lending for corporations and consumers taking place (see Section 1.2.1 on non-bank credit). The main national organisations are the Czech National Bank (CNB) which has the financial supervisory and regulatory role, and the Ministry of Finance (MFCR), which initiates financial legislation and sets the stage for innovation-related projects, such as the feasibility study on the potential of data in financial services in the Czech Republic (see Chapter 2 on the structure of regulation of the financial market in the Czech Republic). The level of digitalisation in the economy for the Czech Republic ranks it 19 out of 27 EU countries in 2022 (European Commission, 2022[3]). Yet, the Czech Republic has been adopting advanced digital measures in the area of payments. Not surprisingly, most of the country's FinTechs operate in this segment.

1.1. FinTech in the Czech Republic: Current state of play

FinTechs are a relatively new type of firms which started emerging on the global scene mostly after 2016 (Shrier and Pentland, 2022[4]; World Bank, 2020[5]).The development of FinTech activity has followed a pattern of constant growth both globally and domestically in the Czech Republic. The COVID-19 pandemic accelerated and intensified the digitalisation trend that pre-existed in the financial markets and increased both the offer and the demand for innovative FinTech solutions. Apart from FinTechs, traditional financial institutions, such as banks and insurance companies, are also active in terms of innovation.

Czech FinTechs mostly provide services in areas such as payments, personal finance management, crowdfunding or Peer-to-Peer (P2P) lending. Open banking applications created on the basis of the Payment Services Directive 2 (PSD2) framework have also been present on the Czech FinTech market, however they have not become as popular (e.g. banks report low customer interest in the multi-banking services they offer). Historically, the Czech Republic has been strong in the payments providers sector, in particular around contactless card payments, where the country has been consistently among the top five countries worldwide in the usage of contactless card payments for the half decade (Visa, 2022[6]).

Prior to the pandemic, the 2017 revenue of Czech FinTechs was estimated to be around EUR 16-31 m (CZK 400–800 m),[1] with long-term forecasts of revenues growing to EUR 205-615 m (CZK 5-15 bn)[2] (Deloitte estimates and forecasts (Deloitte, 2018[7])). On the demand side, there is openness to new digital financial products, services and solutions, and the business sector is relatively quick in adopting financial services innovations (ICLG, 2021[8]).

There are 113 Czech FinTech companies in the country active across a large number of different sectors of regulated and unregulated activity (FinTech Cowboys, 2022[9]) (see Figure 1.1). There is no harmonised definition of FinTech sectors of activity in OECD countries, and the market may use different terminologies for the definition or categorisation of FinTech activities and firms. In this report, the systematic approach used for the classification of FinTech activity stems from the Czech National Bank license categories and has been enriched to also include FinTech activities that do not require a license under the Czech regulatory framework.

Figure 1.1. Czech FinTech activity mapping

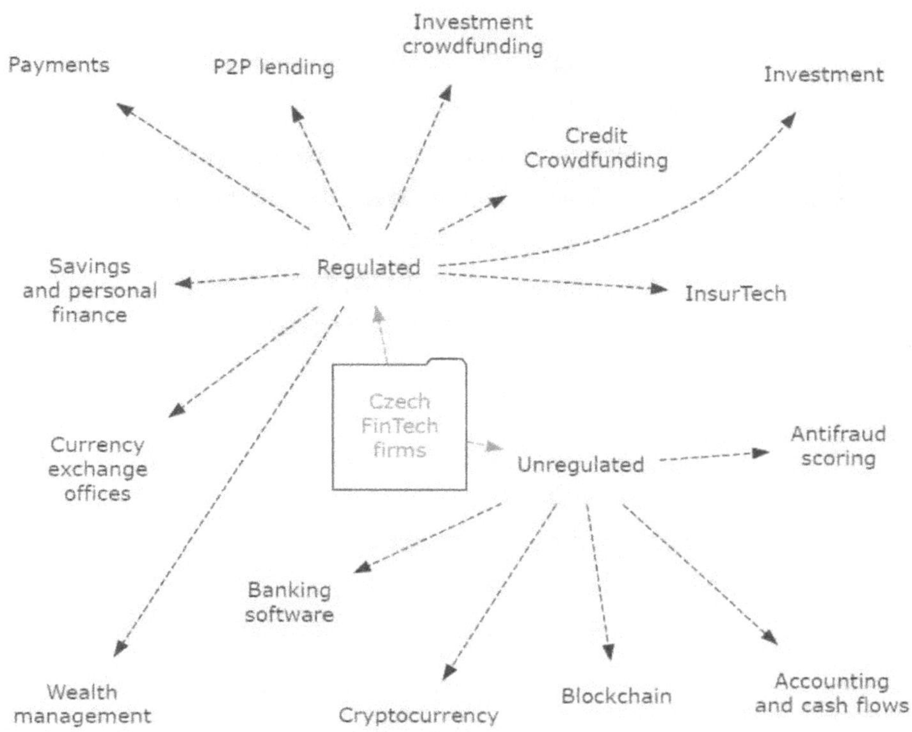

Source: OECD analysis and (CNB, 2022[10]).

1.2. FinTechs' main areas of operation

Czech FinTechs are active in many sectors of financial market activity. The most represented areas in terms of number of companies are accounting, payments, savings and personal finance, P2P lending and crowdfunding (Figure 1.2). Many Czech FinTech companies provide services similar to other globally successful FinTechs (for example "buy now, pay later" services – CZ Twisto, SE Klarna).

Figure 1.2. Number of Czech FinTech firms, 2022

As of July 2022

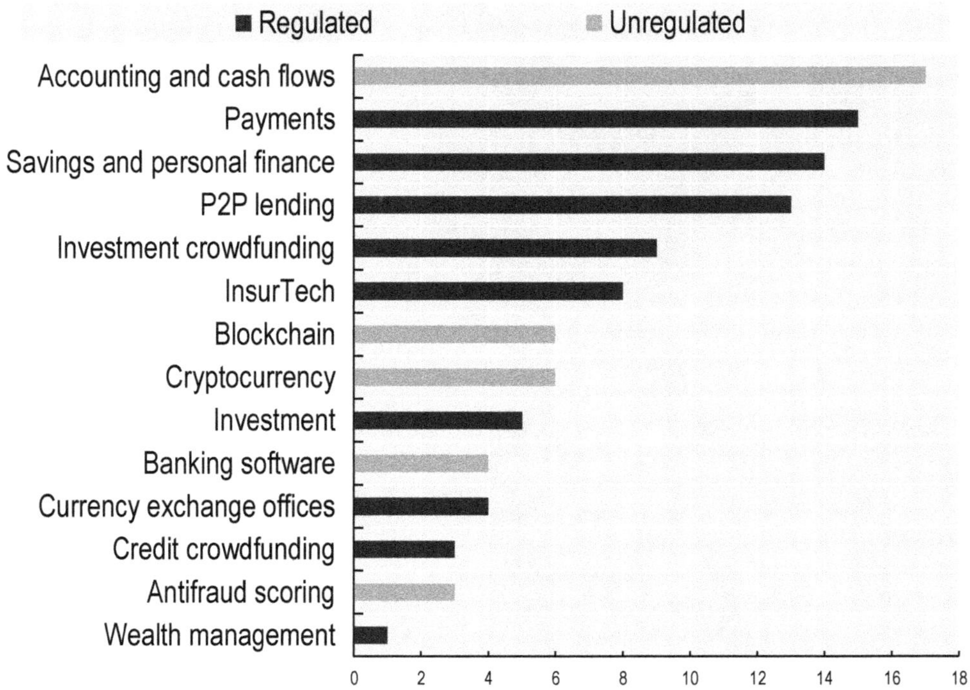

Note: This table does not include additional five foreign FinTechs and two FinTechs operating in unknown category.
Source: OECD construction based on data from FinTech Cowboys (2022[9]), Fintechová mapa České republiky - jaro 2022: přes 100 fintechů, https://fintechcowboys.cz/fintechova-mapa-ceske-republiky-jaro-2022-pres-100-fintechu/.

1.2.1. Non-bank credit

The total balance sheet of non-bank credit providers in 2021 stood at EUR 16.9 bn (CZK 420.2 bn),[3] equivalent to about 5% of the total banking sector credit. The volume of loans granted was EUR 13 bn (CZK 324.8 bn) (MFCR, 2022[11]).[4] The volume of granted loans of financial leasing companies and other lending companies decreased, whereas in the case of factoring and forfeiting, the volume increased by 26.6% (MFCR, 2022[11]).

Non-bank lending is non-trivial in some segments of the private sector, namely the business sector (Figure 1.3). Non-bank lending refers to companies whose main or major business activity involves providing credit or loans (e.g. financial leasing, factoring, consumer credit, hire-purchase financing, etc.), though in fact about 80% of assets of non-bank lenders belong to financial leasing companies. Assets of non-bank credit providers had hovered around 6% of the banking sector's total assets for a long time, but their relative size has been declining in 2019 and 2020 (MFCR, 2021[2]).

Figure 1.3. Loans to non-financial private sector from banks and non-bank financial corporations engaged in lending, 31 March 2022

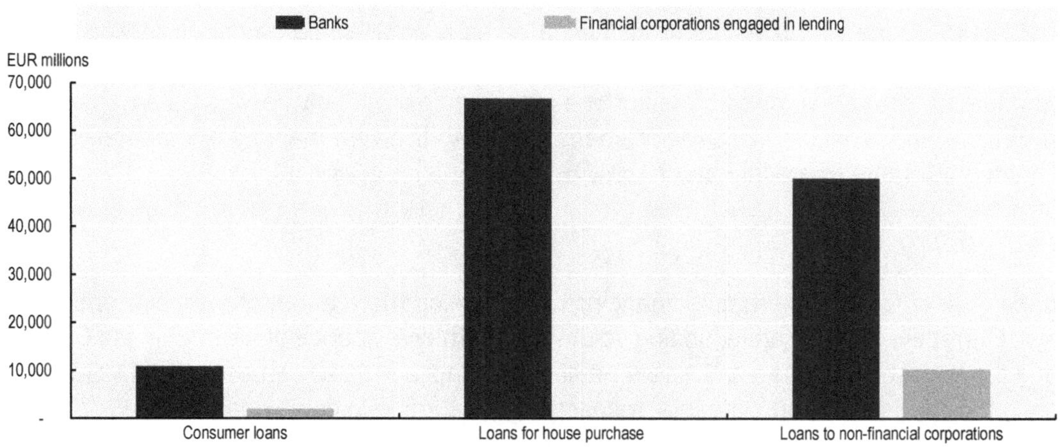

Note: Based on exchange rate as of 31 March 2022.
Source: ARAD time series database of the CNB.

Overall credit levels to the private sector in the Czech Republic are low compared with OECD countries. There is therefore potentially room for growth for credit facilitated by FinTechs (Figure 1.4). Innovative lending platforms have indeed experienced a boom in the last few years, especially in the fields P2P consumer lending and crowdfunding platforms. One of the possible reasons for that might be the persistently low interest rates offered by banks for current as well as savings accounts for a substantial part of the last decade which led customers to invest their funds in one of these services rather than just saving them in their accounts.

Figure 1.4. Total credit to the non-financial sector, 2021

Percentage of GDP

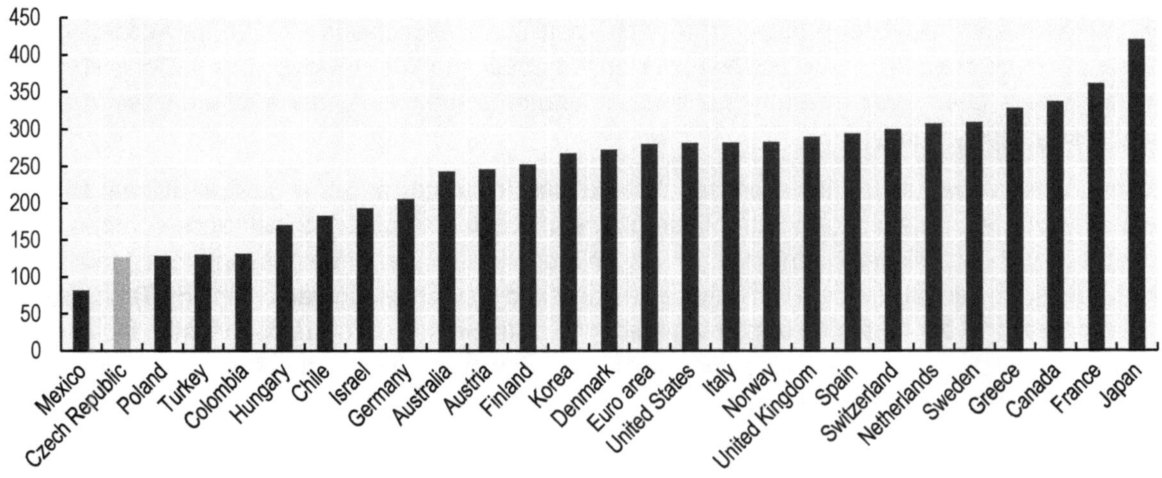

Source: BIS credit statistics

P2P lending platforms

Some of the biggest FinTechs in the Czech Republic in terms of number of customers or valuation are P2P lending platforms. FinTechs seeking to operate P2P lending platforms must obtain an authorisation from the CNB to operate as a payment institution or as a small-scale payment service provider, if no exemptions set forth in the Act on Payments apply (see Section 2.2.4). That is the case if they do not provide the loans themselves, or on behalf of one of the parties, but only serve as a payment intermediary between debtors and creditors. This requirement applies to the vast majority of companies offering P2P loans (Thomson Reuters Practical Law, 2020[12])

Crowdfunding

Crowdfunding, as a form of alternative financing, is becoming more and more popular among the Czech population. Currently, the per capita funding volume of alternative finance platforms[5] in the Czech Republic are among the lowest in Europe – USD 12.91 million per capita in 2020 compared with USD 125, 114 and 90 million in Latvia, Estonia and Lithuania, respectively, according to survey data (CCAF, 2021[13]). Overall crowdfunding volume amounted to USD 138.3 million in 2020, however this volume is twofold compared with 2019. Some 14 platforms operate in the country. Although only three are local, 90% of alternative lending volume stems from local based platforms (CCAF, 2021[13]).

Regulatory changes, following the EU framework, are underway for this sector in the Czech Republic; loan-based and investment crowdfunding will become subject to legal regulation and supervision by the CNB (must obtain a license by 10 November 2023) (see further in Section 2.2.6). Crowdfunding service providers will now be subject to similar regulatory requirements as, for example, securities dealers, investment intermediaries, or payment service providers. The regulation will apply if the crowdfunding is intended for a business project of a value that does not exceed EUR 5 million threshold. In case of donation crowdfunding or crowdfunding services provided to project owners who are consumers, the regulation does not apply. Experts believe that the regulation will increase the attractiveness of this type of investment and that there will be a significant increase in investment through crowdfunding platforms (Advokátní deník, 2022[14]).

1.2.2. InsurTech

Recently, the Czech InsurTech Association was formed to bring together InsurTech companies, represent their interests and facilitate a support (Czech InsurTech Association, 2022[15]). According to this Association, there are a few InsurTech solutions on the Czech market. However, this sector is small. Some InsurTechs have been established by traditional insurance companies under a different brand name (for example iMutuMutu, CubiQ).

The Czech Insurance Association assesses that the local insurance sector is quite traditional and heavily regulated with a strong aversion to risk. Therefore, some of the established insurance companies prefer co-operation with established partners which are, in their view, a guarantee of a long-term stability, rather than start-ups. The usual co-operation between established insurance companies and FinTechs is focused more on operational support (chat bots, image recognition technologies, systems for estimation of damage amounts), rather than on direct insurance solutions. However, this perspective is shifting and more co-operation between FinTech and insurance companies can be expected.

1.3. FinTechs co-operation and competition with the banking sector

There are no specific regulatory barriers preventing FinTech businesses from co-operating and entering into arrangements with traditional financial services providers (except for the requirements applicable to specific services such as bank outsourcing rules).[6] However, the traditional financial services providers prefer established, well-known sellers (especially in core banking systems, customer relationship management and trading platforms) when searching for new digital solutions or improvements to their current offerings. Anecdotal evidence by Czech FinTechs suggests that traditional financial service providers can be considered to be averse to change, which is perhaps justified by their dominant position in the Czech financial services market (Thomson Reuters Practical Law, 2020[12]). However, this is evolving and even though banks have been historically rather reluctant to co-operate with FinTechs, they are starting to focus more on better user experience to ensure greater customer loyalty and more user-friendly, cheaper services to retain clients amid increasing competition in the market driven by FinTechs. To that end, some Czech banks have established accelerator programs[7] for FinTech start-ups or operate corporate venture capital funds. Additionally, banks acquire participations in FinTech's equity or entire FinTech companies with a view to benefitting from the innovative product or technological solution offered by the FinTech company and improve their core services. Examples include mobile banking or personal finance management.[8] As a result, the level of overall digitalisation of the Czech banking sector and the availability of new innovative solutions or products offered by banks have improved significantly throughout the past decade.

In order to provide some context, it can be noted that the overall start-up ecosystem in the Czech Republic (including but not restricted to FinTech firms) comprises currently about 1 000 active start-ups, three unicorns (companies valued at over USD 1 bn), and approximately 100 successful exits for a total amount exceeding EUR 12 bn (CZK 292.8 bn).[9] According to the same source, there was EUR 222.3 m (CZK 5.5 bn)[10] invested into start-ups in the first half of the year 2022. Start-ups are also generally an important and constantly growing source of job opportunities in the Czech Republic. In 2019, approximately 90 000 people were working in start-ups, double the number of start-up employees in 2017 (Czech Founders, 2022[16]).

1.3.1. Project SONIA: APIs and Bank Identity (Project SONIA) potential drivers of innovation in the Czech financial services sector

PSD2 lays down the legal basis for open banking, and was implemented into the Czech legislation by law No 370/2017 Coll., Act on Payments (MFCR, 2017[17]) that went into effect during 2018. Banks are therefore required to provide qualified payment-service providers (PSPs) connectivity to access customer account data and to initiate payments, following consent by the account owner, but only "*to the extent they* [information about the user's payment account] *are accessible to the user via the Internet*" (MFCR, 2017[17]). The connectivity is usually offered by setting up an Application Programming Interfaces (APIs). Anecdotal evidence by some FinTechs operating in the Czech Republic suggests that they experience technical issues and other challenges that prevent them from connecting directly to the banks' APIs on a regular basis. FinTechs have reported that banks limit access to the minimum scope of data required by law. That might in some cases be due to banks' other legal requirements or because of upholding the bank secrecy obligation. Often, FinTechs operating in this sector and requiring payment account information from users, turn to aggregators, an intermediary, to provide them the data collected through APIs.

API aggregators are being used to address the abovementioned issue and provide single access to payment account data after it has been gathered from different banks, each through its own API. There are currently two aggregators operating in the Czech financial market, the privately-owned Bank APIs Aggregation Platform (BAAPI) called Trask, and Finbricks / Multibank open banking aggregation platform, owned by KB SmartSolutions, a subsidiary of KB bank. Trask aggregates transaction history and balances of ten Czech banks,[11] and offers similar service for the Slovak Republic and Hungarian banks. Furthermore, Trask offers payment initiation service (PIS) from any Czech bank and services based on the aggregated data, such as customer financial profiling and customer identity verification. All the aggregated data available through Trask are GDPR (i.e. EU General Data Protection Regulation) compliant (Trask, 2022[18]). Finbricks provides access to basic banking operations, such as payment requests or transaction history through a single interface. Apart from that, Finbricks also offers access to other financial products via the interface, such as BankID, distributed payment or payment gateway. (Finbricks, 2022[19]).

In parallel, the Czech Banking Association introduced a Czech Standard for Open banking, which aims at a uniform implementation of the PSD2 API standard in the Czech market. However, the standard is not mandatory, so it is up to the discretion of individual banks to decide whether they want to adhere to the standard or not. Moreover, in some cases, it is even possible to deviate from the standard within the scope of the specific information system of the bank since these vary significantly among different banks (Czech Banking Association, 2022[20]).

The bank identity initiative, "Bank ID", is another initiative in the Czech financial sector which falls under e-government activities. Bank ID is operated by the company Bankovní identita, a.s., which is owned by nine Czech banks.[12] This method of digital verification of identity was built upon the API framework (see Section 2.2.5). Bank ID users can log in to the portals of various companies and state administration with their bank electronically confirming their legal identity. When verifying their identity with Bank ID, users must first log in to their online banking. If the log-in is successful, the users are further redirected to a special website where they agree to the transfer of data and are then redirected back to the original portal as verified by the bank identity. Only the banks hold the users' personal data and only the users can determine where, how and for what purpose they want to use the identity verification (Bank ID, 2022[21]).

Some of the public administration services that can be accessed using the Bank ID include the vehicle register or the land registry, the ability to complete and submit tax returns, apply for certain social benefits, find out the amount of one's pension, download vaccination certificates or medical prescriptions. Apart from public administration services, Bank ID can be also used for verifying identity for a commercial use. The identity can be commercially used, for example accessing client zones or applications, filling in forms, verifying and confirming data or transactions, or digitally signing documents. It is also being used to verify identity when entering into a contract with some private companies in fields such as energy or finance. This service is free for consumers because the payment obligation for the service belongs to the commercial entity and not to the customer. The Bank ID tool has been widely adopted in the Czech Republic; as of May 2022, 2, Bank ID was used as a digital identity verification at least once on public administration portals by 1.1 million users (about 10% of the population of the Czech Republic) and over 220, 000 users (about 2% of the population) identified themselves at more than 100 private companies which are using Bank ID. Many more public sector participants, mobile operators and some universities are expected to join (mostly health insurance companies, universities and mobile operators) by the end of 2022.

Box 1.1. The proposed amendment to eIDAS and its possible impact on Bank ID

The proposed amendment to the electronic IDentification, Authentication and trust Services (eIDAS) regulation could have a significant impact on provision of financials services, especially offline functionality of the proposed European Digital Identity Wallets, according to CNB officials. The amended version of the regulation envisages the use of "European digital ID wallets" which will enable EU citizens to authenticate and access online public and private services across the EU.

The preferred option for eIDAS amendment is expected to have a positive impact on innovation, international trade and competitiveness, to contribute to economic growth and lead to additional investment in digital identity solutions (European Commission, 2022[22]). What is more, the proposed amendment to this regulation would make the local Bank ID project subject to modifications, to fit the framework that would apply to the European Digital Identity, but ultimately undermining the unique position Czech banks have secured in providing identity-based access to private and public services. The entry into effect of the amendment across the EU is expected in 2030

References

Advokátní deník (2022), "Crowdfunding se nově zařadí mezi běžné investiční nástroje", https://advokatnidenik.cz/2022/04/28/nova-zakonna-regulace-zaradi-crowdfunding-mezi-bezne-investicni-nastroje/ (accessed on 4 August 2022). [14]

Bank ID (2022), *Your digital ID Bank identity*, https://www.bankid.cz/en (accessed on 30 June 2022). [21]

CCAF (2021), *The 2nd Global Alternative Finance Market Benchmarking Report*, CCAF, https://www.jbs.cam.ac.uk/faculty-research/centres/alternative-finance/publications/the-2nd-global-alternative-finance-market-benchmarking-report/ (accessed on 25 January 2022). [13]

CNB (2022), *ARAD - Time Serie System - Czech National bank*, https://www.cnb.cz/cnb/STAT.ARADY_PKG.STROM_DRILL?p_strid=0&p_lang=EN (accessed on 4 August 2022). [1]

CNB (2022), *Regulated institutions and registered financial market entities lists*, https://apl.cnb.cz/apljerrsdad/JERRS.WEB07.INTRO_PAGE?p_lang=en (accessed on 17 June 2022). [10]

CNB (2011), *Financial Market Supervision Report 2010*, https://www.cnb.cz/export/sites/cnb/en/supervision-financial-market/.galleries/aggregate_information_financial_sector/financial_market_supervision_reports/download/fms_2010.pdf (accessed on 24 August 2022). [24]

Czech Banking Association (2022), *Czech standard for Open banking Czech Banking Association*, https://cbaonline.cz/cesky-standard-pro-open-banking (accessed on 30 June 2022). [20]

Czech Founders (2022), *Startupy a Stát*, https://www.slideshare.net/VitHorky/startupy-a-stt-report-czech-founderspdf?from_action=save (accessed on 4 August 2022). [16]

Czech InsurTech Association (2022), *czechinsurtech.cz*, https://www.czechinsurtech.cz/en/ (accessed on 29 August 2022). [15]

Deloitte (2018), *FinTech v ČR i ve světě Vliv nových technologií na finanční sektor*, https://www2.deloitte.com/content/dam/Deloitte/cz/Documents/financial-services/FinTech_v_CR_i_ve_svete_v2.pdf (accessed on 22 August 2022). [7]

European Commission (2022), *Czech Republic in the Digital Economy and Society Index | Shaping Europe's digital future*, https://digital-strategy.ec.europa.eu/en/policies/desi-czech-republic (accessed on 11 August 2022). [3]

European Commission (2022), *EUR-Lex Proposal for a REGULATION OF THE EUROPEAN PARLIAMENT AND OF THE COUNCIL amending Regulation (EU) No 910/2014 as regards establishing a framework for a European Digital Identity- 52021PC0281 - EN - EUR-Lex*, https://eur-lex.europa.eu/legal-content/EN/TXT/?uri=CELEX%3A52021PC0281 (accessed on 29 July 2022). [22]

Finbricks (2022), *FINBRICKS MULTIBANK - ALL BANKS IN ONE PLACE*, https://www.finbricks.com/index_en.html (accessed on 31 October 2022). [19]

FinTech Cowboys (2022), *Fintechová mapa České republiky - jaro 2022: přes 100 fintechů*, https://fintechcowboys.cz/fintechova-mapa-ceske-republiky-jaro-2022-pres-100-fintechu/ (accessed on 4 August 2022). [9]

ICLG (2021), *Fintech Law and Regulations, Czech Republic 2021-2022*, https://iclg.com/practice-areas/fintech-laws-and-regulations/czech-republic (accessed on 17 June 2022). [8]

MFCR (2022), *Report on Financial Market Developments in 2021*, https://www.mfcr.cz/assets/en/media/2022-08-17_Report-on-Financial-Market-Developments-in-2021_v02.pdf (accessed on 21 September 2022). [23]

MFCR (2022), *Report on Financial Market Developments in 2021 (in Czech)*, https://www.mfcr.cz/assets/cs/media/2022-06-30_Zprava-o-vyvoji-financniho-trhu-v-roce-2021_v02.pdf (accessed on 4 August 2022). [11]

MFCR (2021), *Report On Financial Market Developments In 2020*, http://www.mfcr.cz/en (accessed on 1 July 2022). [2]

MFCR (2017), *Act No 370/2017 Sb. on Payments*, https://www.mfcr.cz/assets/cs/media/Zak_2017-370_Zakon-o-platebnim-styku-anglicky-preklad-k-1-4-2019.pdf (accessed on 24 August 2022). [17]

Shrier, D. and A. Pentland (2022), *Global Fintech: Financial Innovation in the Connected World*, MIT Press, https://books.google.com/books?hl=en&lr=&id=fLxNEAAAQBAJ&oi=fnd&pg=PA1&dq=Shrier,+David+and+Alex+Pentland.+2022.+%E2%80%9CGlobal+Fintech:+financial+innovation+in+the+connecting+world,%E2%80%9D+no.+ISBN+9780262543668.&ots=w_S5PR1HW7&sig=6BVfvWpfwPCagJ_KHh80wNofocA (accessed on 3 August 2022). [4]

Thomson Reuters Practical Law (2020), *FinTech in the Czech Republic: overview*, https://uk.practicallaw.thomsonreuters.com/w-014-8515?transitionType=Default&contextData=(sc.Default)&firstPage=true#co_anchor_a559060 (accessed on 4 August 2022). [12]

Trask (2022), *Trask – BAAPI – enabling innovation*, https://www.trask.cz/en/baapi (accessed on 12 August 2022). [18]

Visa (2022), *Contactless Payments Around the Globe*, https://www.visa.com.bs/visa-everywhere/innovation/contactless-payments-around-the-globe.html (accessed on 31 October 2022). [6]

World Bank (2020), "How Regulators Respond To FinTech : Evaluating the Different Approaches – Sandboxes and Beyond", *Fintech Note*, No. 4, https://doi.org/10.1596/33698. [5]

Notes

[1] Based on exchange rate as of 31 December 2017 which was CZK 25.54 for EUR 1.

[2] Based on exchange rate as of 14 July 2022 which was CZK 24.4 for EUR 1.

[3] Based on exchange rate as of 31 December 2021 which was CZK 24.860 for EUR 1.

[4] The MFCR has made the Report on Financial Market Developments in 2021 available in English as well (MFCR, 2022[23]).

[5] All funds raised via an online digital marketplace, including P2P/marketplace lending (debt-crowdfunding), balance sheet lending, equity-crowdfunding and non-investment crowdfunding.

[6] The outsourcing rules for certain financial institutions are set not only by local regulation, but also by EU law and binding guidelines from European regulators (EBA, EIOPA). In some cases, the regulator must be notified, in other cases the outsourcing is not allowed at all. CNB has for example issued a Communication on the EBA's general guidelines on outsourcing or introduced principles of outsourcing cloud services.

[7] The three biggest the Czech banks each have their own version of accelerator programs.

[8] Example of banks which acquired in past few years either partially or wholly the following FinTechs: Komerční banka – Lemonero, Upvest, Roger, FinBricks; Airbank – Zonky; Česká spořitelna – wflow.com, Inwestown; ČSOB – MALL Pay.

[9] Based on exchange rate as of 14 July 2022 which was CZK 24.4 for EUR 1.

[10] Based on exchange rate as of 30 June 2022 which was CZK 24.74 for EUR 1.

[11] Česká Spořitelna, ČSOB, Moneta, Airbank, Equa, Creditas, Komerční banka, Raiffeisen Bank Czech, Raiffeisen Bank Romania, and J&T Bank.

[12] The shareholders are Air Bank, Česká spořitelna, ČSOB, Fio banka, Komerční banka, mBank, Moneta Money Bank, Raiffeisenbank and UniCredit Bank.

2 The structure of financial regulation and supervision in the Czech Republic

This chapter analyses the structure of financial regulation, focusing on the Ministry of Finance of the Czech Republic which is responsible for drafting legislation to regulate the capital market, and the Czech National Bank (CNB) which is the financial market supervisory authority. Historically the CNB had a technology-neutral approach to supervision but in 2019, it established a FinTech contact point to help resolve unclear regulatory issues. The CNB has been facing elevated demand for authorisation for payment service providers, expressing in parallel, dissatisfaction with the quality of applications submitted. The licensed number of payment service providers has been in fact declining. The CNB is expected to start supervising crowdfunding activity following Regulation 2020/1503 of the EU after completion of the national legislation process. The future implementation of the Regulation of Markets in Crypto Assets (MiCA) is expected to further expand CNB's supervisory scope.

2.1. The Ministry of Finance of the Czech Republic: the regulatory authority for financial markets

The MFCR is responsible for developing the financial market policy and drafting legislation governing the financial market. The MFCR is the central government authority responsible for the financial market, the regulation of the issuance of electronic money and the protection of consumer interests in the financial market, with the exception of the supervision of the financial market which lies within the scope of the CNB's competence. In addition, the MFCR is responsible for the contribution to building savings and state contribution to supplementary pension insurance etc. The MFCR performs regular capital market analyses and ensures the Czech membership in the international financial institutions and bodies of the European Union in the capital market area (MFCR, 2022[1]).The MFCR has many additional roles on top of its responsibilities with regard to the financial market in the areas of fiscal policy, taxes etc.[1]

In terms of organisational structure, Section 07 of the MFCR is responsible for financial markets, with responsibilities divided among three departments: Department 27 - Financial Markets I, Department 35 - Financial Markets II and Department 36 – Financial Markets III (MFCR, 2022[2]). The specific responsibilities of each of the departments are outlined below.

Department 27 is involved in formulating policy proposals for issues related to the systemically important financial intermediaries, financial stability and resolution. It carries out legislative activities in the banking sector, building societies / home-purchase savings, cooperative savings, financial market oversight and financial stability and ensures its harmonization with EU law, and represents the Czech Republic in European Commission and EU Council working groups and committees in relation to legislative bills within the area of its competence. Department 35 formulates policy proposals in the area of capital markets, payment services, cash circulation, currency exchange, market infrastructure, insurance sector and private pension savings products. As part of its mandate, Department 35 formulates strategic proposals, impact and comparative studies, proposals for substantive solutions, proposals for substantive intents of bills including evaluations of new or amended regulation's impacts and ensures that these are consulted within internal and external consulting procedure. Department 36 operates in the field of consumer protection in financial services (including promoting financial education), consumer credit and intermediation and the build-up of savings. It drafts methodologies for the performance of supervision and the related guidelines for enforcing fulfilment of obligations and administrative sanctions. It formulates proposals, determines the purpose, defines the assignment of and changes to information systems that are managed and operated by the Ministry for the purposes of supervision, processing of applications for state support for building savings and state contributions to supplementary pension insurance and supplementary pension savings and their returns and changes in the data on participants. Within the scope of its competence, it prepares strategic proposals, impact and comparative studies, proposals for substantive solutions, proposals for substantive intentions of laws and draft legal regulations, including regulatory impact assessments, and ensures their discussion in internal and external consultation proceedings ((MFCR, 2022[2]) and bilateral meetings of OECD team with MFCR officials).

2.1.1. Financial education

The MFCR is the responsible authority for promoting financial education in the Czech Republic. It is responsible for creating the policy and concept of financial education and preparing strategic proposals; managing the Working Group for Financial Education, comprising representatives of other Ministries; providing regular measurements of the level of financial literacy of the adult population and acting as a professional consultant in the implementation of financial education in educational programs for schools. The CNB is an independent professional consultant to the Working Group for Financial Education and acquaints the public with the basic principles of the functioning of the economy, money circulation, financial markets and supports or runs financial education activities (MFCR, 2022[3]).

In 2019, the MFCR published an extensive report assessing the level of financial literacy in the Czech Republic, by different sectors. The report highlighted low level of financial instruments uptake (demand) by the domestic SME sector (MFCR, 2019[4]). Following the policy and action recommendations included in the report, the MFCR introduced in 2021 a website called "Capital Guide"[2], designed for SMEs to make them more familiar with financing tools. The website was developed in cooperation with the European Commission and co-funded by the European Union's Structural Reform Support Programme. The website includes examples of various local FinTech financing solutions such as crowdfunding, equity and lending platforms.

In 2020, the MFCR conducted a survey on the level of financial literacy among Czech adults (MFCR, 2020[5]) and in the same year published a National Strategy on Financial Education (MFCR, 2020[6]) (for more on the survey and the National Strategy see Chapter 4).

National Strategy for the Development of the Capital Market

Also in 2019, the MFCR introduced the National Strategy for the Development of the Capital Market in the Czech Republic 2019 –23. In this Strategy, approved by the Czech Government in 2019, it is stated that the Czech capital markets fail to sufficiently fulfil the function of efficient allocation of unutilised savings towards enterprises who need funding and that the banking system prevails. The Strategy for market development called, among others, for more diversity in the SME financing offering with alternatives to bank financing and subsidies from the European Union, as well as greater support for innovation in finance (MFCR, 2019[7]).

With regard to the regulatory approach, the Strategy stresses the need to remove unnecessary regulatory burdens and costs, except for those that draw from the requirements of EU law. In addition, regulatory stability was highlighted as important. When adopting regulatory changes affecting the capital market, the following basic principles were noted: consultation of changes with regulated entities, description and argumentation for changes, proportionality of changes targeted to market failures, and minimization of other changes unless explicitly required by regulated entities. The abolition of existing regulation should not be avoided a priori, and adoption through accelerated legislative process has to be avoided (MFCR, 2019[7]).

2.2. Czech National Bank: the unified financial markets supervisory authority

The Czech National Bank (CNB) is the sole unified supervisory authority for the financial markets in the Czech Republic.[3] The CNB therefore supervises the banking sector, the capital market, the insurance industry, pension funds, credit unions, bureaux-de-change and non-bank payment provider. In cooperation with the MFCR, which is responsible for the preparation of laws in the financial market area, the CNB participates in the preparation of primary legislation and lays down secondary rules in the form of decrees and measures of a general nature; it authorises, regulates, supervises and, issues penalties for non-compliance with these rules (CNB, 2022[8]). It is worth noting that the CNB has no official mandate with regard to fostering competition in the financial sector.

The current mandate of the CNB as sole unified supervisory authority was established in February 2006, when the Czech Parliament passed the Financial Market Supervision Integration Act.[4] On 1 April 2006, under this Act, the CNB took over all the activities of the Czech Securities Commission (CSC), the Finance Ministry's Office of the State Supervision in Insurance and Pension Funds (ÚDPP) and the Office for Supervision of Credit Unions (ÚDDZ), which all ceased to exist as of that date.

According to CNB officials, the CNB Board approves CNB's decisions and policies. All proposals for the Board are formally circulated to all relevant departments before submission to the Board for comments and amendments. If consensus cannot be found neither on the level of executive directors, nor by Board member responsible for oversight of respective departments, disagreements are highlighted and left for the Board to be decided.

The CNB shall take a position on proposals presented to the Government for consideration that concern the fields of its competence (this is detailed in the Rules of Procedure of the Government - Art II.[5], and in the Legislative Rules[6]), and that it shall act in an advisory capacity vis-a-vis the Government in matters of monetary and macroprudential policy and the financial market (Art. 10) (as set forth by Act No. 6/1993 Coll.). The Minister of Finance or another nominated member of the Government may attend the meetings of the CNB Board in an advisory capacity and may submit motions for discussion, while the Governor of the CNB, or a Deputy Governor nominated by him, may attend the meetings of the Government in an advisory capacity (Art. 11).

The CNB, together with the MFCR, shall prepare and submit to the Government draft legislation on the currency and the circulation of money, and draft legislation concerning the status, competence, organisation and activities of the CNB, save for financial market supervision, the payment system and electronic money issuance.[7] The CNB shall also cooperate with the MFCR in preparing draft legislation in the areas of financial markets, payment system, electronic money issuance, foreign exchange management and the adoption of the single currency, the euro, in the Czech Republic. The details of this cooperation are set out formally in a memorandum from 2006.[8]

At the European level, the CNB is involved in the three European financial market supervisory authorities established on 1 January 2011, namely the European Securities and Markets Authority (ESMA), the European Banking Authority (EBA) and the European Insurance and Occupational Pensions Authority (EIOPA), as well as the European Systemic Risk Board (ESRB for macro-prudential policy relating mainly to systemic risks). At the international level as the supervisory authority, it is involved in the International Organization of Securities Commissions (IOSCO), the International Association of Insurance Supervisors (IAIS), the International Organisation of Pension Supervisors (IOPS), the International Monetary Fund (IMF), the Bank for International Settlements (BIS), and the European Central Bank (ECB) (CNB, 2022[9]).

2.2.1. The CNB's internal structure

The set-up of financial market supervisory activities involves several departments within the CNB. The "gate keepers" are the Licensing and Enforcement Department which carries out licensing, approval and authorisation activities (i.e. first-instance proceedings and decision-making on license, permit and approval applications). After a successful authorisation, this department continues to be of relevance to market participants as it also conducts enforcement activities including first-instance proceedings and decision-making on licence, permit and approval revocation and on the cancellation of registration. In addition, the Licensing and Enforcement Department supervises public offerings of investment securities, supervising compliance with the duties of issuers of listed securities, and supervising regulated market operators, settlement systems with settlement finality of central counterparties, multilateral trading systems and central depositories (CNB, 2022[10]).

The functions of supervision are separated between two departments – Financial Market Supervision Department and Financial Market Supervision Department II. The first department is responsible for the supervision of large institutions, whose activity is likely to affect financial stability (credit institutions, insurance and reinsurance corporations, pension management companies, the central depository, central counterparties and non-financial contracting parties of OTC derivatives, operators of settlement systems with settlement finality and operators of investment instrument markets, as well as foreign entities similar to this list in respect of their activities in the Czech Republic). The second department is responsible for the supervision of the smaller entities, in particular entities offering payment services and electronic money, financial intermediaries, all consumer credit provision (i.e. including by banks). The responsibilities of supervision include off-site and on-site prudential, consumer protection and AML/CFT supervision (CNB, 2022[10]). Decision-making in supervisory work is separated from the CNB Board's decision-making. In this sense, the CNB Board does not interfere in the decision-making process at the supervisory level. The CNB Board is regularly informed about supervisory activities, primarily with the aim of assessing the effectiveness of the work of the first-instance authority (CNB, 2022[9]).

The CNB separates the drafting of regulations, any decision-making around licensing, enforcement proceedings and activities relating to resolution and macro-prudential policy (financial stability) from the direct performance of supervisory activity. The main components of the functional organisation of supervision are prudential supervision, business conduct supervision and AML/CFT supervision. These activities must be coordinated to prevent conflicts arising between their different approaches and to ensure that they support other activities and thereby contribute to meeting the CNB's supervisory objectives (CNB, 2022[9]). According to CNB officials, cooperation between CNB departments is promoted through formal and informal committees or working groups, as well as through ad hoc cooperation, where appropriate (considering the confidentiality of supervisory information) and as necessary.

The procedures for submitting applications for permission or approval to the CNB are governed by the relevant sector-specific laws and by decrees issued by the CNB to implement the individual laws. The laws are prepared by the MFCR and, in some cases, the Ministry of Justice. The decrees issued by the CNB stipulate the specific requisites of applications, the specimen forms on which applications should be submitted, and the annexes that must be attached to applications (CNB, 2022[11]).

2.2.2. The CNB's supervisory approach

The CNB seeks to apply a single approach to individual financial market entities. To this end, it organises its supervisory activities not on a sectoral but on a functional basis. The CNB's objective in the area of supervision, as defined by law, is to ensure financial stability and the safe and sound operation of the financial system in the Czech Republic, contributing to achieving its primary objective - price stability. The main components of the functional organisation of supervision are prudential supervision, conduct of business supervision and also AML/CFT supervision.

a. Supervisory activity

In all its supervisory activities, the CNB applies a risk-based approach based on a risk assessment system (RAS). This means that it allocates the largest proportion of its resources to areas that are systemically the most important or the most risky (CNB, 2022[9]). The structure of the supervision unit in the CNB reflects the importance of safeguarding financial stability as the primary objective: At the decision of the CNB Board, the organisation of the CNB's supervisory work was updated as of 1 March 2017 and supervision is currently performed by the Financial Market Supervision Department and the Financial Market Supervision Department II. The Financial Market Supervision Department conducts off-site and on-site supervision of credit institutions, insurance and reinsurance corporations and pension funds, three sectors that are defined systemically important by the CNB. The Financial Market Supervision Department II conducts off-site and on-site supervision of payment and electronic money institutions, investment, insurance and credit intermediaries, bureaux de change, non-bank investment firms, management companies, non-bank consumer credit and others, sectors not defined as systemically important[9] (CNB, 2022[9]). With regards to regulatory manpower, the structure of the supervision function implies that while the Supervision Department oversees several dozens of institutions, the Supervision Department II oversees thousands of entities.

The nature of supervision and its conduct differ between systemically important institutions and those that are not defined as such: The CNB meets the senior managers of systemically important institutions on a regular basis and communicates with middle managers on an ongoing basis. The CNB focuses its supervisory attention mainly on sectors and institutions which are systemically important or have the potential to be systemically important due to the size of the impact of their potential failure (CNB, 2022[9]). In its supervisory work, the CNB's supervisory unit takes into account the conclusions and recommendations of the financial stability unit, which are contained primarily in the Financial Stability Report.

The CNB is responsible for macro prudential supervision of the financial system[10]. The unit at the CNB responsible for financial stability and macroprudential policy comes under the broader remit of financial market supervision. Legally binding instruments are available to be applied to entities regulated and supervised by the CNB. The CNB mostly applies macro prudential tools to the banking sector though macroprudential policy also covers non-banking components of the financial system. The CNB assesses the activities and position of non-bank financial institutions on an ongoing basis and, where necessary, responds to changes in systemic risk and resilience (CNB, 2020[12]) (for more extensive description of CNB's actions and available tools with regard to macroprudential policy see Annex B).

Supervising non-systemically important institutions: the case of non-bank consumer lending providers

Traditionally the CNB has opposed to acting as supervisor for non-systemically important institutions; in 2014, when consultations on a new national Act on Credit for Consumers were taking place, "strong disagreement was expressed [by the CNB to the Ministry of Finance consultation paper] with the extension of the scope of the Act to business loans and with the CNB becoming a supervisory authority for the provision and distribution of credit for consumers, as non-bank loans are not relevant to systemic stability and the central bank's mandate. The CNB has also long been against extending the applicability of prudential regulation to non-bank loan providers. It should therefore not license or supervise the distribution of non-bank loans." According to the CNB, non-bank consumer lending providers are not entities which accept deposits or manage the funds of third parties and whose failure has serious consequences for clients, investors or financial stability (CNB, 2015[13]). In 2015, the CNB restated its disagreement with the integration of supervision of non-bank consumer credit providers and intermediaries into the CNB stating that "there is no link to the CNB's statutory objectives, there is a risk of monetary financing without compensation of the CNB's supervisory costs, such integration brings no positive effects, and there are no grounds for prudential supervision of such entities" (CNB, 2016[14]). Eventually, the MFCR insisted the CNB be designated as the supervisory authority for non-bank consumer credit providers, and it has been their supervisor since the Act on Consumer Credit[11] went into effect in end of 2016. Currently, the CNB claims that "in some cases, these are companies (consumer credit providers) which are assessed as systemically important" (CNB, 2022[9]). At the end of 2020, the CNB supervised 85 non-bank consumer credit providers (CNB, 2021[15]).

Supervision is broken down according to whether it takes the form of on-site or off-site surveillance. With continuous supervision, applicable to systemically important institutions, the main emphasis is placed on off-site supervisory activities. On-site surveillance focuses on prudential, conduct of business and AML/CFT inspections. On-site presence of supervisors in banks, insurance companies and credit unions is considered an important component of the conduct of supervision, whereas in non-systemically important sectors supervision relies more heavily on off-site surveillance, regular reporting and complaints from the public (CNB, 2022[9]). Closer inspection might occur for important institutions in non-systemically important sectors, but otherwise inspection in non-systemically important sectors is based on a reactive approach (CNB, 2022[9]).

The CNB considers complaints from the public as an important source of information about the approach of supervised entities to clients, especially in the case of credit and payment institutions, bureaux de change and insurance companies. Findings obtained when investigating submissions made by the public are used as a basis for thematic surveys in the sector concerned and to identify supervised entities to be included in the on-site inspection. Naturally, given the dominance of the banking sector in the provision of financial services, it is the sector with the highest amount of complaints, followed by insurance firms and non-bank credit providers

Figure 2.1. Submissions from the public to the CNB, by sectors

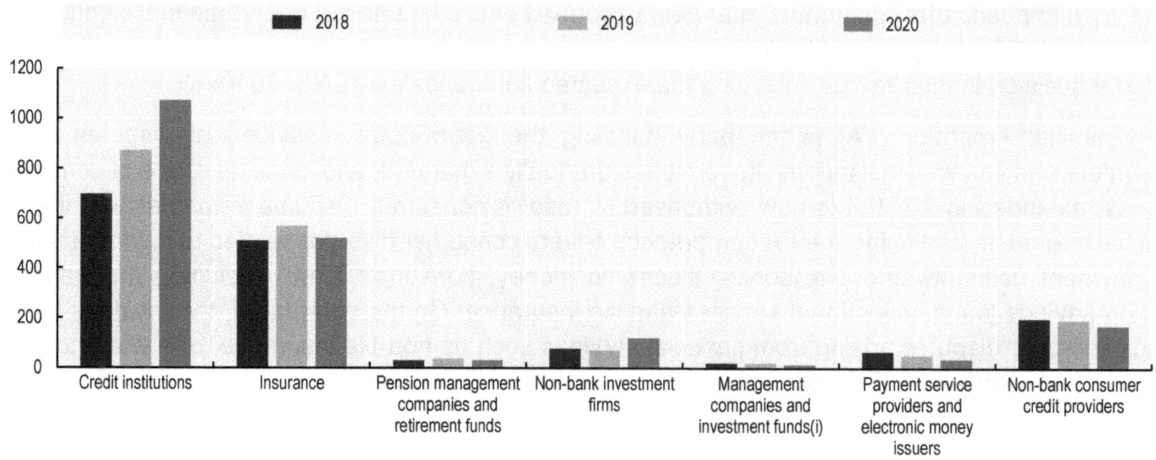

Note: (i) including similar foreign entities
Source: CNB (2021[15])

The CNB measures the effectiveness of its work not only by evaluating its results with respect to its objectives, but also by measuring the costs that it and supervised entities incur. The CNB supervisory unit decides about the allocation of its capacity, chooses relevant supervisory procedures and instruments, and communicates its requirements to supervised institutions and other supervisory authorities based on the results of risk assessments.

b. Supervision in the area of business conduct

The objective of business conduct supervision is to contribute to increasing the transparency of the financial market and to resolving any systemic shortcomings in the areas of conduct of business and professional care. Business conduct supervision primarily involves the protection of retail clients' or consumers' interests. An identical supervisory approach is applied to all institutions to a similar extent and complexity of activities based on the principle of proportionality (CNB, 2022[9]). Act No. 36/2008 Coll., which amended and extended Act No. 634/1992 on Consumer Protection, promulgated on 12 February 2008 has fundamentally affected the CNB and entrusted it with the supervision of compliance with consumer protection rules by regulated financial market entities (CNB, 2009[16]). Following the act, the CNB was entrusted with supervising compliance with the prohibition of unfair commercial practices, the prohibition of discrimination against consumers and with obligations regarding the provision of proper pricing information in respect with entities subject to its supervision[12] (CNB, 2009[16]). Consumer protection is usually performed subsidiarily to the rules set out in the relevant sectoral legal regulations (CNB, 2022[9]). The CNB follows sectoral product oversight governance rules (e.g. EBA's Guidelines on product oversight and governance arrangements for retail banking products[13]).

In addition, the CNB oversees compliance with the obligations stipulated by the Civil Code, in force since 2014, for concluding contracts on financial services concluded at a distance by telephone, fax, e-mail or the Internet. The Civil Code sets out in detail the scope of information that must be provided to the consumer before concluding the contract (MFCR, 2022[17]).

Supervised institutions have no disclosure duty in the area of consumer protection. The supervisory authority obtains information on possible breaches of the relevant legal rules from complaints filed either by consumers or by consumer protection associations under Article 26 of the Consumer Protection Act and from its own activities (CNB, 2010[18]). As the public financial market supervisory authority, the CNB is not entitled to intervene in private legal relationships between supervised institutions and consumers and is therefore not an out-of-court dispute settlement authority. This means that its consumer protection activities differ markedly from those of, say, the Financial Arbitrator (CNB, 2010[18]). Consequently, it sometimes happens that consumers after being informed of this fact do not cooperate sufficiently with the CNB during the investigation of their complaints, since for them the CNB's supervisory activities will not lead to a decision in their favour, including the expected compensation (CNB, 2010[18]).

The Financial Arbitrator (FA) is the body handling the out-of-court resolution of disputes between consumers and financial institutions. Its remit has gradually expanded, and since its scope of competence was last extended in 2022, it is now authorised to resolve consumer disputes across almost the entire financial market. In particular, the FA competence covers consumer disputes related to payment services, non-payment accounts and passbooks, electronic money, consumer loans, including mortgages and building savings loans, investment services and life insurance. On the other hand, the FA does not have jurisdiction over disputes arising from financial services such as non-life insurance, and shareholder and bondholder disputes (MFCR, 2022[19]).

c. Anti-Money Laundering and Counter-Terrorism financing (AML/CFT) compliance

The aim of supervision in the area of AML/CFT carried by the CNB is to contribute to enhancing internal control mechanisms in relevant entities by assessing the system of internal principles for this area and conducting thematic sector-wide surveys. On an individual basis, it involves performing off-site supervision of relevant entities in the AML/CFT area identified in complaints from the public. In on-site inspections, the CNB focuses on checking compliance with the AML/CFT legislation with the aim of verifying the functioning and effectiveness of the system of AML/CFT measures of and to determine whether the measures are sufficiently robust and effective to prevent exploitation for money laundering and terrorist financing (CNB, 2022[9]). These inspection take place with cooperation with the Financial Analytical Office, the responsible agency for AML/CFT compliance in the Czech Republic (see Section 2.3).

In 2020, Act No. 527/2020 was adopted as an amendment to Act No. 253/2008 Coll., on Certain Measures against Money Laundering and Terrorist Financing, and Act No. 300/2016 Coll., on the Central Register of Accounts. The amendment o of the Act No. 37/2021 Coll., on the Register of Beneficial Owners was also finalised. The aim of the proposals is to transpose an amendment of the Anti-Money Laundering Directive and incorporate the recommendations of the MONEYVAL Committee.[14] The amendment introduces, for example, an explicit duty to carry out intensified vetting of clients in higher-risk situations, an increase in the maximum penalties applicable, an extension of the data recorded in the Central Register of Accounts, and a clarified definition of beneficial owner. The changes apply to all "obliged entities", i.e. almost all financial market undertakings (CNB, 2021[15]).

d. Financial literacy

The CNB has participated in several projects in recent years aimed at raising financial and economic literacy in the Czech Republic, with a focus on school pupils. In particular, it has made publicly available several teaching materials for school teachers. The latest initiative of the CNB was the creation of the CNB Visitor Centre (CNB, 2022[20]).

2.2.3. The CNB's approach towards innovation in finance

The CNB has historically maintained its approach toward innovation in finance, and that is of technology neutral supervision. The CNB states that business activity in the financial market is governed by sector-specific Acts,[15] which also lay down conditions for the performance of individual activities, including their authorisation and registration requirements. All providers of relevant products and services must comply with those conditions regardless of the innovative aspects of those activities, according to the CNB. If an innovative activity or service does not meet the criteria of a regulated activity, the entity offering it is subject to neither supervision nor registration by the CNB.[16] As such, the CNB does not keep a register of FinTech companies, but includes regulated FinTech entities performing a regulated activity under its register (CNB, 2018[21]).

Crypto-assets

When it comes to crypto-assets, the CNB does not currently consider them as money or funds as defined in Act on Payments and instead classifies them as intangibles. The law arguably permits Czech banks to offer crypto-related services as long as they comply with AML regulations though there is an indirect limitation regarding trade of tokens. The Czech Republic has, however, implemented a stricter legal model than AMLD5 requiring that every crypto-related firm be regulated by the Czech government, not only exchanges and wallets as the EU regulation stipulates. Gains on crypto-asset investments are taxed at rates between 15% and 19% (Thomson Reuters, 2022[22]). A trading license is required to conduct business in the area of crypto-assets and that can be obtained from the Trade Licensing Office (within the Ministry of Industry and Trade).

FinTech contact point at the CNB

Nonetheless, in November 2019, the CNB established a FinTech contact point. The contact point aims at helping resolve unclear regulatory issues - including licensing and supervisory ones - so as to facilitate compliance with the duties imposed on enquirers by financial market regulations. Opinions of the CNB provided via the contact point do not substitute for authorisations or approvals granted in licensing proceedings and are not binding in any way (CNB, 2022[23]). The FinTech contact point is currently operated by a team of 2 CNB staff members and receives/handles on average approx. 2-3 requests per month The capacity of the FinTech contact point is further limited by the very broad agenda of the financial innovations team, as all innovation and digitalisation issues go through this same team.

In the future it is expected that more financial activities carried out by FinTechs will become regulated across the EU, starting with crypto asset providers following the imminent agreement on the Regulation of Markets in Crypto Assets (MiCA) and the DLT pilot regime (see Section 3.1 for more details on on-going and expected regulatory initiatives at the EU), which will increase the demand for authorisation by the CNB even further. Future inquiries related to forthcoming regulation are expected to be more standard qualified questions that require a different, much more resource intensive effort to be resolved. Such processes are also expected to be much lengthier (up to three months) than replying to a FinTech query received through the Contact Point.

2.2.4. Supervision in the area of payment services providers

In 2010, the CNB's supervisory responsibilities were extended to include non-bank payment services providers and non-bank electronic money issuers.[17] The newly regulated entities comprised payment institutions, electronic money institutions, small-scale payment services providers and small-scale electronic money issuers.[18]

The current Act on Payments[19] is the national legislation from 2017 implementing the Directive on Payment Services in the Internal Market (PSD2). The Act introduced numerous new duties for existing holders of authorisation to provide payment services and provided for the establishment of new types of entities. Entities which were originally subject to simple registration (i.e. small-scale payment service providers and small-scale electronic money issuers) were now authorised in licensing proceedings, similarly to payment institutions and electronic money institutions (CNB, 2019[24]).

Small-scale payment service provider licence might be applicable if the average monthly amount of payment transactions it has executed in the previous 12 months does not exceed EUR 3 million and if services are offered in the Czech Republic (MFCR, 2017[25]). A similar option exists for licences for issuing electronic money. However, in essence, the geographical limitation is hard to follow through and customers can be foreign residents. The small scale licence allows providers to offer limited payment services under less burdensome operating conditions; whilst a payment institution is required, among others, to have initial capital, organizational capacity and professional experienced directors, small-scale payment providers are exempt from these requirements, and instead need only to have a security and operating risk management system and a system for handling user complaints in place (MFCR, 2017[25])[20].

The new payment services that were introduced by the Act on Payments include indirect submission of a payment order (payment initiation service (PIS)) and provision of information on a payment account (account information service (AIS)). In addition to payment institutions, a new type of entity – a payment account information administrator – able to provide information on a payment account – was introduced (CNB, 2019[24]) and (MFCR, 2017[25]).

Payment institutions and electronic money institutions had to adapt their governance systems to the new requirements, in particular their operational and security risk management systems, their complaints systems, their business resumption and continuity procedures and their procedures for submitting, monitoring and recording sensitive payment data (including classification of and access to sensitive data). Payment institutions and electronic money institutions also had to demonstrate that part of their payment services business was pursued in the Czech Republic. During the transition stage to full compliance with the new requirements, CNB supervisory assessments identified frequent deficiencies in operational and security risk management systems and related business resumption and continuity procedures. The main shortcomings detected in the course of off-site surveillance related to the calculation of payment institutions' eligible capital, breaches of the statutory cap on the monthly average amount of payment transactions for small-scale payment service providers, and discrepancies in data on the value and investment structure of funds entrusted by users to payment service providers in order for the latter to execute payment transaction (CNB, 2019[24]).

The CNB regards the supervision of payment and electronic money institutions as an integral part of maintaining the stability of the financial system in the Czech Republic. This means in particular supporting the sound development, market discipline and competitiveness of the supervised institutions, preventing systemic crises and strengthening public confidence in the financial system (CNB, 2022[26]).

The supervision of payment institutions includes decisions on licence, permit and registration applications and prior approvals pursuant to special legal rules; inspection of adherence to the conditions stipulated in licences and authorisations; inspection of adherence to laws, insofar as the CNB has the power to conduct such inspections under the law or special legal rules; inspection of adherence to the decrees and provisions issued by the CNB; collection of information needed to perform supervision and its enforcement, and verification of whether it is true, complete and up-to-date; the imposition of remedial measures and penalties; and proceedings regarding administrative offences (CNB, 2022[26]).

The CNB has been facing elevated demand for authorisation for the various payment entities since 2018 ((CNB, 2020[27]; 2021[15]). In parallel, the CNB has been expressing dissatisfaction with the quality of applications submitted: "Compared with other sectors, the quality of applications here is often low. The CNB thus has to call on the applicants repeatedly and in detail to bring their internal regulations into conformity with their business plan and the legislation. Applicants were also often unable to submit an account agreement with a credit institution or a promise to enter into an agreement demonstrating in the licensing proceedings that the funds entrusted for the performance of payment transactions were protected" (CNB, 2020[27]). In the following year the CNB mentioned that applicants in the payments sector had difficulties describing their business plans for the purpose of authorisation (CNB, 2021[15]).

Since the enactment of the Act on Payments, the number of non-bank payment service providers, both small and "regular", has been declining according to CNB statistics. In particular, the amount of small payment service providers, which did not require a licence prior to 2018, has sharply declined (Figure 2.2).

Figure 2.2. Summary of regulated and registered payment and electronic money institutions in the Czech Republic

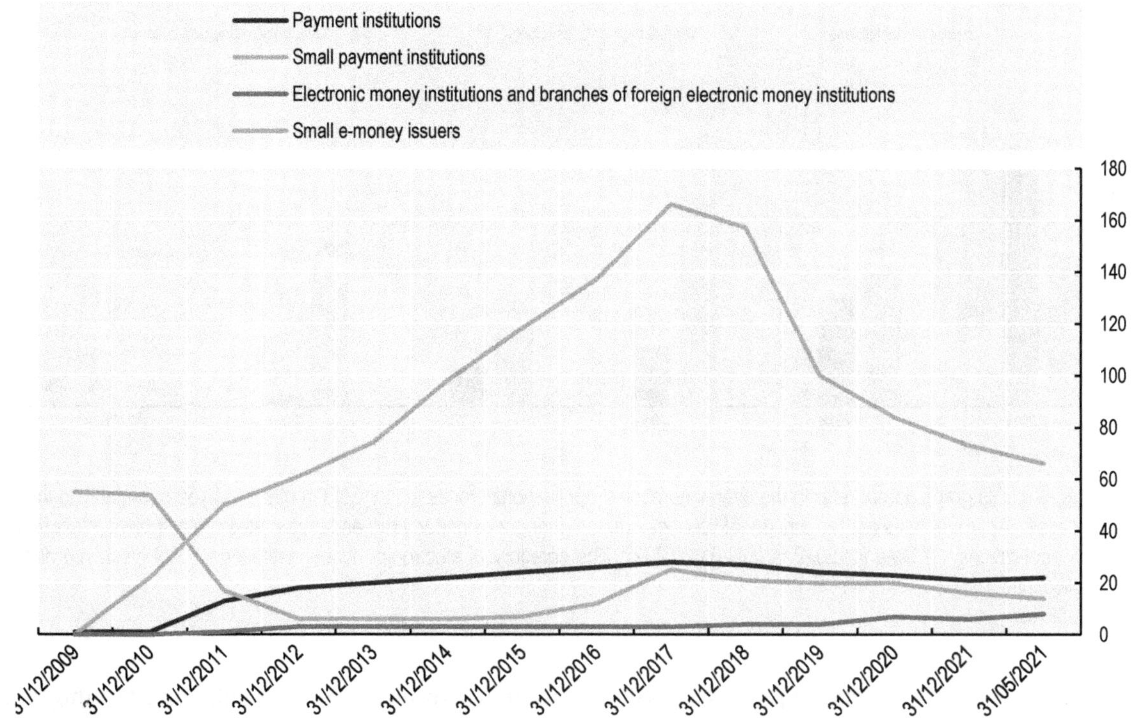

Source: CNB (2022[28]), Regulated institutions and registered financial market entities lists, https://apl.cnb.cz/apljerrsdad/JERRS.WEB07.INTRO_PAGE?p_lang=en.

In addition, the incidence of suspended proceedings or rejected applications in the payments sector has been higher than in other financial market sectors (CNB, 2021[15]). In 2020, decisions were taken on 47 applications (seven permits were issued, 32 proceedings were discontinued and eight applications were rejected). Overall approval ratios have been quite low in the payment sector in the past several years (Figure 2.3). In addition to low approval rate of new licences, enforcement measures against payment providers have also been substantial; in 2020, the CNB revoked licenses in 13 cases due to enforcement proceedings under the Act on Payments (CNB, 2021[15]). In 2019 licences were revoked in 22 cases (three small-scale electronic money issuers, 18 small-scale payment service providers and one payment institution). A large proportion of the licence revocations were the result of failure to demonstrate compliance with the conditions for operation under the new Act on Payments (CNB, 2020[27]).

Figure 2.3. Licencing approval rates by the CNB in the payments sector

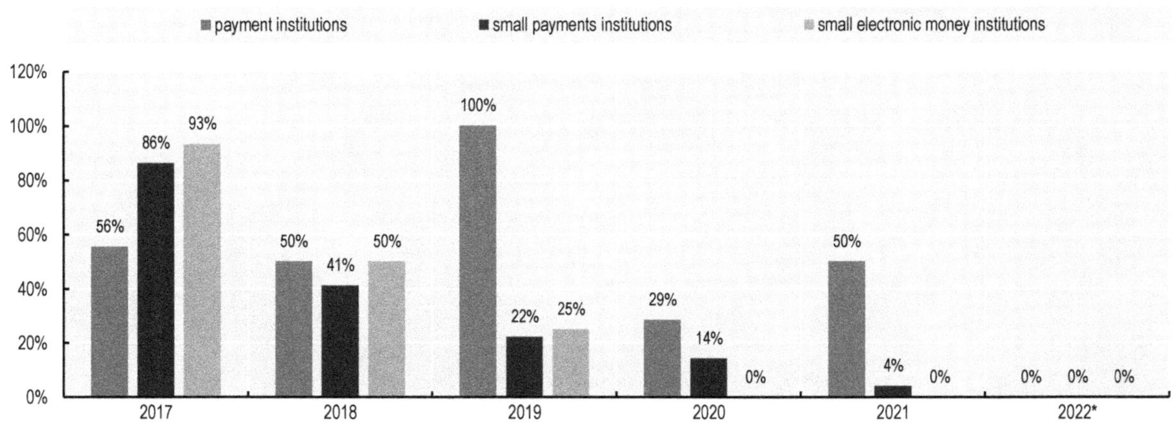

Note: Percentages in this graph do not refer to the overall number of applications processed by CNB in observed years, but only to the subset of terminated cases. Approval rates are the amount of licences granted during a calendar year, and these rates are complementary to refused and withdrawn applications. (*) Data for 2022 is until 31/05/2022. The category of electronic money institutions is not displayed due to low amount of applications.
Source: CNB officials.

Timelines for licence approvals for payment institutions and for small payment institutions are the longest compared with other types of licenses issued by the CNB, 25 and 18.3 months on average, respectively, in 2021. For comparison, average length of proceedings completed in 2021 for credit institutions and non-bank consumer lenders was 13.1 and 14.1 months respectively. In addition, the application rate for these types of licences, and small-scale payment institution licence in particular, has been high in recent years.

As regards AML/CFT compliance in the payments system, the CNB assessed that a large number of non-bank payment service providers were risky from this perspective in 2020 (CNB, 2021[15]).

As the Act on Payments allows for an exemption for small payment services providers and small e-money issuers, they can only provide their services within the Czech Republic. The CNB has identified this group of entities as having exploited the domestic legislative environment for their foreign business activities, without often having at least minimum ties with the Czech market neither from ownership not from clientele perspectives (CNB, 2021[15]). On-site examinations identified recurring inconsistencies between the business plan submitted in the licensing proceedings and the entity's actual activities and shortcomings arising from the formal regulation of processes and activities in internal rules, which do not correspond to the actual functioning of these entities. These are mainly shortcomings in the protection of clients' funds, compliance with AML/CFT duties and compliance with the reporting duty to the CNB and the information duty to payments service users. The CNB plans to continue to focus on the problematic aspects of this sector in its future supervisory work. Supervision will also focus on monitoring the application of strong customer authentication in electronic card transactions and of exemptions from this duty by payment institutions, electronic money institutions and bank card payments (CNB, 2021[15]).

2.2.5. The Czech Standard for Open Banking, Account Information Service Providers and Bank ID

Following the implementation of the Act on Payments[21] (the local PSD2 legislation) and the requirement that banks provide other qualified payment-service providers (PSPs) connectivity to access customer account data and to initiate payments, an industry-initiated Standard for Open Banking was developed in the Czech Republic (see Section 1.3.1). The Czech Standard for Open Banking was developed by the local banking association, and the recent version, 5.0, became valid in 2022. The standard is voluntary, and it is up to each bank to consider joining it (Czech Banking Association, 2022[29]).

One of the most prominent use cases to have evolved from the implementation of the Standard for Open Banking was the Bank ID (project SONIA) implementation (see Section 1.3.1). The Bank ID is an interface that allows for digital verification of identity. Users of the interface can log in to the portals of various companies and state administration. Once a user logs in to the banking environment she can instruct the bank to send her data to the company or office participating in the arrangements. Seven banks currently provide this service, and it is free of charge for users (Bank ID, 2022[30]). Although in terms of level of service this seems to be an improvement for consumers, this might also be valuable for banks to collect data on their customers as to their commercial habits and to verify the data collected within the identification process in public registries, and even though direct information on the activity of users within the commercial or governmental site is not visible to the validating bank. Furthermore, it also enabled banks to verify the data collected within the identification process in public registries (Basic Public Administration Registers).

The launch of the Bank ID required some legislative amendments. The CNB worked with the MFCR, the Ministry of the Interior and the Financial Analytical Office on amendments to the Act on Banks and the Act on Selected Measures against Legitimisation of Proceeds of Crime and Financing of Terrorism during 2019 and 2020. Besides banking identity, the amendment contains some other changes, for example allowing banks to access data in public administration information systems using their own information systems, and expanding and adjusting this existing right for insurance companies. The amendments were adopted in 2020 (CNB, 2020[27]; 2021[15]; FAU, 2021[31]).[22]

To bring about true "open banking" competition, the PSD2 directive allows access by third party providers (TPPs) to customer data held by credit institutions, and the provision of payment initiation services (PIS) and account information services (AIS). The function and licence requirements for an AIS providers (AISP) operating in the Czech market are laid down in the Act on Payments (MFCR, 2017[25]). Despite the important role of this function in the context of open banking, as of 31 August 2022, only three entities have been authorised by CNB as AISPs under the Act on Payments (2018) (CNB, 2022[28])[23]. This figure has been constant since mid-2019. Apart from three pure AISPs there are four PIS providers (PISPs) who are also AISPs[24] – Akcenta, GoPay, Roger and ZNPay. For comparison, as of March 2022, 97 AISPs operate in the UK, growing quickly from 20 providers only two years earlier (Open Banking UK, 2022[32]).

2.2.6. Supervision of non-bank credit providers

Non-bank providers of *business* credit are not subject to CNB authorisation, or any other financial supervision in the Czech Republic. The Consumer Credit Act (No. 257/2016 Coll.) applies only to all *consumer* credit provided by businesses to consumers and entrusts the CNB with supervision of all consumer credit providers and intermediaries, including the conduct of licensing proceedings, during which compliance with the conditions for granting a licence is examined. The Act specifies in detail the information duties to consumers and some other rights and duties in the area of consumer credit which improve the consumer's position (e.g. the possibility of early loan repayment, the assessment of creditworthiness, restrictions on penalties for overdue loan repayments and restrictions on the exercise of the right of pledge) (CNB, 2017[33]).

2018 saw the end of the transition period enabling non-bank consumer credit providers to apply for a proper license and fulfil the requirements of the Consumer Credit Act thus allowing them to continue their activity. Of the 108 entities that had previously been carrying on business under a trade license, 84 applicants were granted non-bank consumer credit provider licenses. A total of 24 applicants were refused due to failure to comply with the licensing conditions or withdrawal of the application. By the end of 2018, the CNB had also granted three new non-bank provider licenses to entities which previously had not pursued this activity (CNB, 2019[24]).

Before the Consumer Credit Act took effect, the sector of non-bank providers of consumer credit amounted to almost 60,000 trading entities. It consisted of a large group of entities operating across the entire range of services, from companies engaged in the provision of consumer credit secured by property, through leasing and traditional consumer credit, to companies providing micro-loans which were not subject to consumer credit regulation (CNB, 2022[9]). Since the transition period was completed, there are about 85 non-bank credit providers in the Czech Republic (CNB, 2022[28]). Besides consumer credit providers, the segment related to non-bank credit provision includes companies authorised to test the professional expertise of all persons negotiating and assessing consumer credit ("accredited persons") . The currently active and authorised non-bank consumer credit providers have been active for a long time, have standardised procedures for the supply and provision of consumer credit and some have a licence for the pursuit of business of a payment institution (CNB, 2022[9]).

Crowdfunding

Regulation of the EU 2020/1503 (The Crowding Regulation) introduces a new category of crowdfunding service providers, the conditions for the provision of crowdfunding services, and regulates the rules of the crowdfunding platform provider's dealings with customers, i.e. investors and project owners. It distinguishes between two types of crowdfunding - loan-based crowdfunding and investment crowdfunding, i.e. the placement of transferable securities and admitted instruments for crowdfunding purposes (European Union, 2020[34]). The Regulation provides for a transitional period with respect to crowdfunding services provided in accordance with national law expected to end on 10 November 2023 (European Commission, 2022[35]).

If the main investment service provided by the crowdfunding service provider is the acceptance and transmission of orders concerning investment instruments, and the placement of investment instruments and admitted instruments for crowdfunding purposes, without any obligation to subscribe for them, the crowdfunding service provider will need a permit to operate from the CNB. It will not need a licence to operate as a securities broker under the Act No. 256/2004 Coll., on Capital Market Business, which is significantly more administratively demanding to obtain (Bird & Bird, 2022[36]). According to CNB officials, some crowdfunding platforms have been already regulated as payment service providers.

2.2.7. Supervision of investment firms, investment funds and management companies

Under the acts governing activities of capital market participants,[25] the CNB is authorised to issue decrees specifying more detailed conditions for entry to the capital market, prudential rules, rules of conduct towards investors and clients, and market transparency rules (CNB, 2022[37]). The CNB is also charged with development of the capital market, investor protection and encouraging investor awareness[26] (The World Bank, 2017[38]).

The regulations in the investment services area apply to bank and non-bank investment firms (including branches from non-EEA countries), investment intermediaries and tied agents of investment firms and investment intermediaries. To a limited extent these regulations also apply to branches of investment firms from EEA countries (CNB, 2022[39]).

The CNB registered 39 entities holding an investment firm licence (as of 2020), of which 16 were banks and 23 were non-banks. CNB supervision of non-bank investment firms focused on checking compliance with the requirements of the transposition of the MiFID II into Czech law in 2018 (CNB, 2021[15]).

Given persisting problems with the activity of foreign entities providing investment services mainly for high-risk investment instruments, an amendment to the Act on Capital Market Business in 2020 stipulated that foreign investment firms may offer investment services in the Czech Republic only temporary or occasionally without establishing a Czech branch, with the exception of the provision of investment services to professional clients, to whom they can continue to provide services permanently without establishing a branch. Permanent provision of investment services by foreign investment firms to retail clients in the Czech Republic is still possible only through a branch or a tied agent (CNB, 2020[27]).

The CNB registered 37 management companies, two branches of foreign management companies, one primary administrator, 6 depositories, 185 investment funds with legal and 234 mutual funds at the end of 2020 (CNB, 2021[15]). Supervision of management companies and investment funds is concentrated mainly on funds with a potentially significant systemic impact, i.e. primarily collective investment funds managing funds from the public. Inspection work is focused on compliance with the rules of conduct of business for fund management and the configuration of governance systems (CNB, 2019[24]).

In its off-site surveillance of investment fund managers and their administrators, the CNB supervises above all their capital quality, the configuration of governance systems and other prerequisites for doing business. The CNB monitors the situation in the investment funds managed or administered by them mainly in terms of compliance with the conduct of business rules in portfolio management. The CNB regards investor relations, and especially whether the information an investor is to obtain is complete, accurate and up-to-date, as a very important area. CNB supervision is also concentrated on relations with depositaries and distributors, which are a significant component of the fund infrastructure. The depositary function is an essential security element in the investment fund area; depositaries are also very useful as regards compliance with the duties arising from the AML/CFT legislation (CNB, 2019[24]).

2.2.8. Insurance, investment and consumer credit intermediaries (financial product distribution)

The financial product distribution segment is characterised by a high number of entities subject to CNB supervision. The insurance intermediaries sector is the largest segment of the Czech financial market in terms of the number of entities supervised (CNB, 2022[9]). The insurance sector is strongly dependent on the activity of insurance intermediaries, whilst such dependence is less present in the investment sector (CNB, 2022[9]). Off-site supervision of distributers is usually reactive and focuses mainly on compliance with the rules of conduct towards clients in the provision of services and on the configuration and functioning of the governance system. Many investment intermediaries have been authorised to intermediate contracts on supplementary pension savings, which has extended the regulated and supervised activities of individual intermediaries. Several hundred intermediaries are authorised to operate in each of the retail distributing sectors (CNB, 2021[15]).

2.3. The Financial Analytical Office (FAÚ)

The Financial Analytical Office (FAU) is an administrative office, subordinated to the MFCR, with nationwide jurisdiction serving as the financial intelligence unit of the Czech Republic. The Office was established on 1 January 2017 on the basis of the national Act No. 368/2016 Coll.. amending Act No. 253/2008 Sb. on the Selected Measures against Legitimisation of Proceeds of Crime and Financing of Terrorism. The position of the Office is described in more detail in section 29c of Act No. 253/2008 Coll. (FAU, 2022[40])

The local AML Act[27] was most recently amended in 2020 by Act 527/2020 Sb. The main impetus for this legislation was the adoption of Directive (EU) 2018/843 of the European Parliament and of the Council of 30 May 2018[28] (hereinafter referred to as the '5th AML Directive'). The amendment was further intended to reflect both the requirements of the 5th AML Directive and the recommendations of the MONEYVAL Committee set out in the Report from the Fifth Round of the Mutual Evaluation of the Czech Republic on the prevention of money laundering and the fight against terrorist financing (FAU, 2020[41]). Changes affecting all obliged entities have been made to the provisions concerning the customer due diligence, namely the introduction of the enhanced customer due diligence and the extension of possibilities of using remote identification to a wider range of obligated entities.

The amendment to the AML Act changed certain parameters of related processes and pushed online identification a bit further. If the FAU finds malpractice in connection with one of the inspected entities, in addition to the actual correction of the problematic situation, financial sanctions will arise as well; the amount of financial sanctions that can now be imposed is many times higher than before, when the upper limit of sanctions reached CZK 10 m: with the amendment, it is now possible to impose a fine of up to CZK 130 m or more, depending on the net annual turnover or the amount of the unjustifiably gained profit (Deloitte, 2021[42]).

Following latest legislative changes, the Czech Republic has achieved full compliance with six of the forty FATF recommendations constituting the international AML/CFT standard according to the second Enhanced Follow-up Report & Technical Compliance Re-Rating. Minor deficiencies remain in the implementation of twenty-nine Recommendations where it has been found "largely compliant". Five Recommendation (targeted financial sanctions, virtual assets, cash couriers and maintenance of statistics) remain "partially complaint". The Czech Republic has no "non-compliant" ratings (MONEYVAL, 2021[43]).

Supervisory activities of the Financial Analytical Office are exercised by the Supervisory Department of the Legal Division (a department consisting of 7 posts, including HOD) in accordance with Section 35 of the AML Act. The main supervisory activities are the checking of compliance of obliged entities and the conduct of offence proceedings. An important part of the activities of the supervisory staff is also the evaluation of the Systems of Internal Procedures of obliged entities, which must be sent to the FAU in accordance with Section 21 of the AML Act (FAU, 2021[31]).

The inspection plan for 2020 included financial institutions (bank, credit union, small-scale payment service provider, exchange office, insurance company) as well as obliged entities providing non-financial services (FAU, 2021[31]). Similarly, in 2019, account the inspection plan included, in particular, banks, payment institutions, small-scale payment service providers, small-scale e-money issuers. Inspection plans are drawn in cooperation with other supervisory bodies, the CNB in particular, and this cooperation includes in addition joint inspections and meeting of employees from both authorities at managerial and working level. Common offences in 2020 involved payment institutions which were punished for failing to comply with prevention obligations (specifically for failing to deliver their system of internal procedures to the FAU within the statutory deadline). The most frequent offence across all financial institutions examined was the failure to comply with the customer due diligence obligations (FAU, 2021[31]).

Occasionally, the FAU perform systemic inspections which include a larger number of obliged entities of the same type. In 2019 the FAU selected for this purpose virtual assets services providers, because, since 1 January 2017, they have become obliged entities (FAU, 2020[41]).

2.4. Non-Financial relevant Regulators

2.4.1. The Office for Personal Data Protection (ÚOOÚ/DPA)

The supervisory authority for data protection designated by the Personal Data Processing Act of 2019[29] is the Office for Personal Data Protection (DPA, as for Data protection Authority or Úřad pro Ochranu Osobních Údajů – ÚOOÚ – in Czech)). It is an independent central authority of the state administration. It creates room for a new role of the Czech DPA - freedom of information. Sections 5 to 15 of the Act are the Czech specific implementation of the EU General Data Protection Regulation (GDPR). The national Act has a part dealing with processing that does not fall within EU law, for example, where it is related to immigration. Title III of the Personal Data Processing Act sets out the requirements for the processing of personal data for criminal 'law enforcement purposes'. Title IV of the Act defines the National security framework, which is outside the scope of EU law. Title V covers the Czech DPA and its duties, functions and powers plus Title VI - the enforcement provisions (DPA, 2022[44]).[30]

Specific for financial services, Article 12, applicable by banks, provides for their exemption from the obligation to communicate a personal data breach to the data subject pursuant to the GDPR Articles 33 and 34 (according to DPA officials).[31]

There is no formal or informal cooperation framework between the CNB and the DPA, neither on authorisation nor supervision.

The highest-rated risk from a data protection perspective relating to FinTechs in the Czech Republic as was raised by DPA is the lack or insufficient transparency towards data subjects. The DPA highlighted the shortcomings of FinTechs having the role of data controllers not meeting their responsibilities under the GDPR when often contracting with third parties. Due to high cost, FinTechs occasionally fail to fulfil their obligation pursuant to the GDPR Article 14 and to provide to the data subject the legally required information. Mitigating the risk of insufficient supervision over third party activities from the controller (FinTech) part over some components, or the whole process of personal data processing, can be demanding and costly in case of certain projects.

2.4.2. Local Cybersecurity Authority (NÚKIB)

The National Cyber and Information Security Agency (NÚKIB) is an independent central administrative body for cyber security, including the protection of classified information in information and communication systems and cryptographic protection. It was established in 2017 on the basis of Act No. 205/2017 Coll.. Act No 181/2014 Coll. on Cyber Security, which is a horizontal legislation relevant for all regulated sectors including financial sector. Only selected financial institutions are regulated by the Act, and in particular those fulfilling the criteria for identification of the critical infrastructure or the operator of essential services.

The CNB and NUKIB overlap in responsibilities with regard to financial entities and the two agencies coordinate the supervisory activities as they cooperate directly. In May 2022, a memorandum of understanding was signed (CNB, 2022[45]), and there is a general legal obligation to coordinate supervisory activities and to minimise the negative impact of such activities on audited entities. With regard to the expected approval of the Digital Operational Resilience Act (DORA), it is expected that NÚKIB will be involved in incident reporting, handling activities, as well acting as a coordinator in all sectors in the country, according to NUKIB officials.

References

Bank ID (2022), *Your digital ID Bank identity*, https://www.bankid.cz/en (accessed on 30 June 2022). [30]

Bird & Bird (2022), *New crowdfunding legislation in the Czech Republic – what does it mean? - Bird & Bird*, https://www.twobirds.com/en/insights/2022/czech-republic/new-crowdfunding-legislation-in-the-czech-republic (accessed on 29 June 2022). [36]

CNB (2022), *Capital market supervision - Czech National Bank*, https://www.cnb.cz/en/supervision-financial-market/conduct-of-supervision/status-of-supervision/capital-market-supervision/ (accessed on 5 July 2022). [37]

CNB (2022), *CNB and NÚKIB signed a memorandum of cooperation - Czech National Bank*, https://www.cnb.cz/cs/cnb-news/aktuality/CNB-a-NUKIB-podepsaly-memorandum-onbspspolupraci/ (accessed on 29 July 2022). [45]

CNB (2022), *CNB launches FinTech contact point - Czech National Bank*, https://www.cnb.cz/en/cnb-news/press-releases/CNB-launches-FinTech-contact-point (accessed on 20 June 2022). [23]

CNB (2022), *Financial market supervision - Czech National Bank*, https://www.cnb.cz/en/supervision-financial-market/ (accessed on 16 June 2022). [8]

CNB (2022), *Investment firms and investment intermediaries - Czech National Bank*, https://www.cnb.cz/en/supervision-financial-market/legislation/investment-firms-and-investment-intermediaries/ (accessed on 5 July 2022). [39]

CNB (2022), *Licensing and approval proceedings conducted by the Czech National Bank - Czech National Bank*, https://www.cnb.cz/en/supervision-financial-market/conduct-of-supervision/licensing-and-approval-proceedings/ (accessed on 16 June 2022). [11]

CNB (2022), *Long-term supervisory strategy of the Czech National Bank - Czech National Bank*, https://www.cnb.cz/en/supervision-financial-market/long-term-supervisory-strategy-of-the-czech-national-bank/ (accessed on 24 June 2022). [9]

CNB (2022), *Organisational structure - Czech National Bank*, https://www.cnb.cz/en/about_cnb/org-structure/ (accessed on 16 June 2022). [10]

CNB (2022), *Regulated institutions and registered financial market entities lists*, https://apl.cnb.cz/apljerrsdad/JERRS.WEB07.INTRO_PAGE?p_lang=en (accessed on 17 June 2022). [28]

CNB (2022), *Supervision of payment institutions and electronic money institutions - Czech National Bank*, https://www.cnb.cz/en/supervision-financial-market/conduct-of-supervision/status-of-supervision/supervision-of-payment-institutions-and-electronic-money-institutions/ (accessed on 5 July 2022). [26]

CNB (2022), *The CNB's activities to support financial literacy were awarded in an international competition*, https://www.cnb.cz/cs/cnb-news/aktuality/Aktivity-CNB-na-podporu-financni-gramotnosti-oceneny-v-mezinarodni-soutezi (accessed on 31 October 2022). [20]

CNB (2021), *Financial Market Supervision Report 2020*, https://www.cnb.cz/export/sites/cnb/en/supervision-financial-market/.galleries/aggregate_information_financial_sector/financial_market_supervision_reports/download/fms_2020.pdf (accessed on 22 June 2022). [15]

CNB (2020), *Financial Market Supervision Report 2019*, https://www.cnb.cz/export/sites/cnb/en/supervision-financial-market/.galleries/aggregate_information_financial_sector/financial_market_supervision_reports/download/fms_2019.pdf (accessed on 22 June 2022). [27]

CNB (2020), *The CNB's Macroprudential Policy Strategy*, https://www.cnb.cz/export/sites/cnb/en/financial-stability/.galleries/macroprudential_policy/cnb_macroprudential_policy_strategy.pdf (accessed on 6 July 2022). [12]

CNB (2019), *Financial Market Supervision Report 2018*, https://www.cnb.cz/export/sites/cnb/en/supervision-financial-market/.galleries/aggregate_information_financial_sector/financial_market_supervision_reports/download/fms_2018.pdf (accessed on 22 June 2022). [24]

CNB (2018), *Financial Market Supervision Report 2017*, https://www.cnb.cz/export/sites/cnb/en/supervision-financial-market/.galleries/aggregate_information_financial_sector/financial_market_supervision_reports/download/fms_2017.pdf (accessed on 22 June 2022). [21]

CNB (2017), *Financial Market Supervision Report 2016*, https://www.cnb.cz/export/sites/cnb/en/supervision-financial-market/.galleries/aggregate_information_financial_sector/financial_market_supervision_reports/download/fms_2016.pdf (accessed on 29 June 2022). [33]

CNB (2016), *Financial Market Supervision Report 2015*, https://www.cnb.cz/export/sites/cnb/en/supervision-financial-market/.galleries/aggregate_information_financial_sector/financial_market_supervision_reports/download/fms_2015.pdf (accessed on 29 June 2022). [14]

CNB (2015), *Financial Market Supervision report 2014*, https://www.cnb.cz/export/sites/cnb/en/supervision-financial-market/.galleries/aggregate_information_financial_sector/financial_market_supervision_reports/download/fms_2014.pdf (accessed on 29 June 2022). [13]

CNB (2010), *Financial Market Supervision Report 2009*. [18]

CNB (2009), *Financial Market Supervision report 2008*. [16]

Czech Banking Association (2022), *Czech standard for Open banking Czech Banking Association*, https://cbaonline.cz/cesky-standard-pro-open-banking (accessed on 30 June 2022). [29]

Deloitte (2021), *Easier online identification, new obliged entities and higher sanctions. What changes does the amendment to the AML Act bring?*, https://www.dreport.cz/en/blog/easier-online-identification-new-obliged-entities-and-higher-sanctions-what-changes-does-the-amendment-to-the-aml-act-bring/ (accessed on 5 July 2022). [42]

DPA (2022), *About the Czech DPA: The Office for Personal Data Protection*, https://www.uoou.cz/en/vismo/zobraz_dok.asp?id_org=200156&id_ktg=1111&p1=1111 (accessed on 7 July 2022). [44]

European Commission (2022), *COMMISSION DELEGATED REGULATION (EU) …/... of 12.7.2022 extending the transitional period for continuing to provide crowdfunding services in accordance with national law as referred to in Article 48(1) of Regulation (EU) 2020/1503 of the European Parliament and of the Council*, https://eurocrowd.org/wp-content/uploads/2022/07/PART-2022-525322V1.pdf (accessed on 21 September 2022). [35]

European Union (2020), *Regulation (EU) 2020/1503 of the European Parliament and of the Council of 7 October 2020 on European crowdfunding service providers for business, and amending Regulation (EU) 2017/1129 and Directive (EU) 2019/1937*, https://eur-lex.europa.eu/legal-content/EN/TXT/?uri=CELEX:32020R1503 (accessed on 29 August 2022). [34]

FAU (2022), *About us | FAÚ*, https://www.financnianalytickyurad.cz/en/about-us#basic-informations (accessed on 4 July 2022). [40]

FAU (2021), *Act on Selected Measures against Legitimisation of Proceeds of Crime and Financing of Terrorism*, https://www.financnianalytickyurad.cz/files/act-no-253-2008-sb-on-the-selected-measures-against-legitimisation-of-proceeds-of-crime-and-financing-of-terrorism-aml-act.pdf (accessed on 31 October 2022). [46]

FAU (2021), *Annual Report 2020 - Financial Analytical Office of the Czech Republic*, https://www.financnianalytickyurad.cz/files/annual-report-2020-financial-analytical-office-of-the-czech-republic.pdf (accessed on 4 July 2022). [31]

FAU (2020), *Annual Report 2019 - Financial Analytical Office of the Czech Republic*, https://www.financnianalytickyurad.cz/files/annual-report-2019-financial-analytical-office-of-the-czech-republic.pdf (accessed on 4 July 2022). [41]

MFCR (2022), *Basic Information | Capital Market | Ministry of Finance of the Czech Republic*, https://www.mfcr.cz/en/themes/capital-market/basic-information (accessed on 1 July 2022). [1]

MFCR (2022), *Consumer protection supervision*, https://financnigramotnost.mfcr.cz/cs/popis-financniho-trhu/dohled-nad-ochranou-spotrebitele (accessed on 1 July 2022). [17]

MFCR (2022), *Members of the Working Group for Financial Education and their role according to the National Strategy for Financial Education 2.0 (in Czech)*, https://financnigramotnost.mfcr.cz/cs/pro-odborniky/pracovni-skupina-pro-financni-vzdelavani/clenove-a-jejich-role (accessed on 30 June 2022). [3]

MFCR (2022), *Organisation chart | About Ministry | Ministry of Finance of the Czech Republic*, https://www.mfcr.cz/en/about-ministry/organisation-chart (accessed on 1 July 2022). [2]

MFCR (2022), *Report on Financial Market Developments in 2021*, https://www.mfcr.cz/assets/en/media/2022-08-17_Report-on-Financial-Market-Developments-in-2021_v02.pdf (accessed on 21 September 2022). [19]

MFCR (2020), *FINANČNÍ GRAMOTNOST 2020*, https://financnigramotnost.mfcr.cz/cs/pro-odborniky/mereni-urovne-financni-gramotnosti/2020/vysledky-mereni-financni-gramotnosti-20-3286#vysledky (accessed on 5 August 2022). [5]

MFCR (2020), *Národní strategie finančního vzdělávání 2.0*, https://www.psfv.cz/cs/pro-odborniky/strategicke-dokumenty (accessed on 5 August 2022). [6]

MFCR (2019), *Capital Markets Literacy In The Czech Republic*. [4]

MFCR (2019), *National Strategy for the Development of the Capital Market in the Czech Republic for the period of 2019-2023*, https://www.mfcr.cz/assets/en/media/201903-National-Strategy-CZ-Capital-Market.pdf (accessed on 1 July 2022). [7]

MFCR (2017), *Act No 370/2017 Sb. on Payments*, https://www.mfcr.cz/assets/cs/media/Zak_2017-370_Zakon-o-platebnim-styku-anglicky-preklad-k-1-4-2019.pdf (accessed on 24 August 2022). [25]

MONEYVAL (2021), *Czech Republic: improvement in fighting money laundering and terrorist financing - Newsroom*, https://www.coe.int/en/web/moneyval/-/czech-republic-improvement-in-fighting-money-laundering-and-terrorist-financing (accessed on 4 July 2022). [43]

Open Banking UK (2022), *Open Banking Impact Report June 2022 – key insights on adoption and business use - Open Banking*, https://www.openbanking.org.uk/insights/open-banking-impact-report-may-2022-key-insights-on-adoption-and-business-use/ (accessed on 1 September 2022). [32]

The World Bank (2017), *Capital Market Assessment / Market Development Options Czech Republic.* [38]

Thomson Reuters (2022), *Cryptocurrency regulations by country*, https://www.thomsonreuters.com/en-us/posts/wp-content/uploads/sites/20/2022/04/Cryptos-Report-Compendium-2022.pdf (accessed on 29 July 2022). [22]

Notes

[1] The mandate of the MFCR in the area of capital market regulation is laid out by Section 4 (1) of Act no. 2/1969 Coll., on the Establishment of Ministries and Other Central Government Authorities of the Czech Republic.

[2] www.kapitalovypruvodce.cz

[3] in accordance with Act No. 6/1993 Coll., on the CNB

[4] Act No. 57/2006 Coll.,

[5] https://www.vlada.cz/en/jednani-vlady/jednaci-rad-vlady/rules-of-procedure-of-the-government-20989/

[6]https://www-vlada-cz.translate.goog/cz/ppov/lrv/dokumenty/legislativni-pravidla-vlady-91209/?_x_tr_sl=cs&_x_tr_tl=en&_x_tr_hl=cs&_x_tr_pto=wapp

[7] Art. 37 of Act No. 6/1993 Coll.

[8] https://www.mfcr.cz/cs/aktualne/tiskove-zpravy/2006/2006-05-11-tiskova-zprava-5926-5926 (in Czech)

[9] With the exception of insurance intermediation who's systemic importance consists in its impact on the stability of the insurance market

[10] The CNB's mandate for conducting macroprudential policy is laid down in Act No. 6/1993 Coll., on the Czech National Bank

[11] Act No. 257/2016 Coll.

[12] On the basis of an amendment to Act No. 634/1992 Coll., on the Consumer Protection Act, and an amendment to Act No. 6/1993 Coll. on the Czech National Bank.

[13] https://www.eba.europa.eu/guidelines-on-product-oversight-and-governance-arrangements-for-retail-banking-products

[14] Committee of Experts on the Evaluation of Anti-Money Laundering Measures and the Financing of Terrorism, a permanent monitoring body of the Council of Europe

[15] Act No. 21/1992 Coll., on Banks, Act No. 277/2009 Coll., on Insurance, Act No. 256/2004 Coll., on Capital Market Undertakings, Act No. 370/2017 Coll., on Payments and Act No. 257/2016 Coll., on Consumer Credit, for example.

[16] Ibid.

[17] This was the result of the adoption of the Payment System Act (No. 284/2009 Coll.,), transposing Directive 2007/64/EC (PSD I) on payment services in the internal market, which took effect in the Czech legislation on 1 November 2009.

[18] The transition period for entities that provided payment services or issued electronic money based on previous authorisations (e.g. entities with foreign exchange licences, credit card credit providers, entities carrying on the business of company savings banks, and mobile operators) ended on 30 April 2011.

[19] Act No. 370/2017 Coll., that took effect on 13 January 2018.

[20] If the payment institution licence is to apply to indirect payment order service or payment account information service, the applying entity is required in addition to have an insurance contract or a comparable guarantee in place. In contrast, small PSPs cannot provide open banking services (AIS / PIS).

[21] Act No. 370/2017 Coll.,

[22] Act No. 49/2020 Coll., which the CNB helped to prepare, amended Act No. 21/1992 Coll., on Banks, and Act No. 253/2008 Coll., on Certain Measures against Money Laundering and Terrorist Financing.

[23] Apart from three pure AISPs there are four PISPs who are also AISPs – Akcenta, GoPay, Roger and ZNPay.

24 Akcenta, GoPay, Roger and ZNPay. Except for ZNPay, all have been licenced before the Act on Payments (2018).

25 The activities of capital market participants are governed mainly by Act No. 256/2004 Coll., on Capital Market Business, as amended, and Act No. 240/2013 Coll., on Management Companies and Investment Funds, as amended.

26 Article 2 of the Act on Supervision of Capital Market, Act No. 15/1998 Coll.

27 Act No. 253/2008 Coll. on Selected Measures against Legitimisation of Proceeds of Crime and Financing of Terrorism.

28 Which amended Directive (EU) 2015/849 of the European Parliament and of the Council of 20 May 2015 on the prevention of the use of the financial system for the purpose of money laundering or terrorist financing and amended Regulation (EU) No 648/2012 of the European Parliament and of the Council and repealed Directive 2005/60/EC of the European Parliament and of the Council and Commission Directive 2006/70/EC and amended Directives 2009/138/EC and 2013/36/EU.

29 No. 110/2019 Coll. – implementing the EU General Data Protection Regulation (GDPR) framework (Directive 2016/680) in the Czech Republic.

30 The Czech DPA is vested with additional powers related to special issues and anchored in special laws. The basic procedural acts are the Supervisory Procedure Act (No. 255/2012 Coll.) and the Administrative Code (Act No. 500/2004 Coll.). Sec. 11 of the Basic Registers Act (No. 111/2009 Coll.) provides that the Czech DPA generates source identifiers of physical persons and item-related identifiers of physical persons, maintains lists thereof, and ensures transfers of a physical person's item-related identifier within one administrative dossier to item-related identifier of this physical person under another dossier on the basis of a legal request (DPA, 2022[44]).

31 Additional aspects of the legal framework applicable to the processing of personal data of financial services customers in the Czech Republic is represented by the following pieces of legislation: Act No. 89/2012 Coll., the Civil Code, Act No. 634/1992 Coll., on consumer protection, Act No. 253/2008 Coll., on AML/CFT, Act No. 21/1992 Coll., on banks, Act No. 6/1993 Coll., on the Czech National Bank, Act No. 370/2017 Coll., the payment services act and Act No. 250/2017 Coll., on electronic identification.

3 Enabling environment for FinTech innovation in the Czech Republic and EU

EU initiatives in the FinTech sector are instrumental for the development of the Czech FinTech market. Some of these relevant initiatives are related to access and use of data, the revision of Payment Services Directive 2, the Regulation of Markets in Crypto-assets and Artificial Intelligence Act proposals, and the establishment of regulatory sandboxes. The Czech FinTech sector has a solid background of industry-led initiatives and a supporting enabling environment. Young Czech start-ups lack sufficient funding sources because of limited development of capital markets and scarce venture capital availability, which is in line with many OECD economies. There is an openness towards new digital financial products or services, and both the business sector and financial consumers are relatively quick in adopting financial innovations. The demand side scores well in basic digital skills. However the country lacks ICT specialists. The Ministry of Finance has published a National Strategy on Financial Education.

3.1. European frameworks and initiatives supporting FinTech innovation

FinTech companies that combine innovative business models and technology to enable, enhance and disrupt financial services have a strong position amongst European Tech companies. Indicatively, four out of the top ten of Europe´s most valuable Tech companies in 2021 were FinTechs (i5 invest, 2022[1]). Based on the same source, nearly EUR 26 billion was invested into FinTech in Europe in 2021 through more than 750 financing deals, sometimes multiple rounds per company, with the biggest single investment reaching approx. EUR 900 m.

The European Union has been consistently supportive of FinTech and actively works towards supporting its safe development. In 2018 the European Commission adopted an action plan on FinTech (European Commission, 2018[2]) to foster a more competitive and innovative European financial sector, enable innovative business models to scale up at the EU level and support the uptake of new technologies such as blockchain[1], artificial intelligence, and cloud services in the financial sector. The main object of the Action plan on FinTech was to enhance supervisory convergence toward technological innovation and prepare the EU financial sector to better embrace the opportunities brought by new technologies.

Building upon the Action plan on FinTech, the European Commission introduced in 2020 the Digital Finance package which came as the result of public consultations and outreach. The package consisted of a Digital Finance Strategy, a Retail Payments Strategy, and legislative proposals for an EU regulatory framework on crypto-assets and proposals for an EU regulatory framework on digital operational resilience. The goal was to foster competition in a financial market, enhance supervisory convergence, support the access to innovative financial products and prepare the financial sector to better embrace the opportunities brought by new technologies, all while ensuring consumer protection and financial stability (European Commission, 2020[3]). The Digital finance strategy aimed to further support the digital transformation of the financial sector by enhancing the digital operational resilience by mostly focusing on removing fragmentation in the Digital Single Market, adapting the EU regulatory framework to facilitate digital innovation or by promoting data-driven finance. All that while trying to mitigate the associated risk and ensure a level playing field among providers of financial services by implementing the principal of same activity, same risk, and same rules. Those initiatives were designed to unleash European innovation and create opportunities to develop better financial products for consumers.

The most recent EU initiative in the field of digital finance is the EU Digital Finance Platform, which was announced in the EU Digital Finance Strategy of 2020 as one of the key actions (European Commission, 2022[4]). The EU Digital Finance Platform is a website which is supposed to foster a dialogue between innovative financial firms and supervisors in order to overcome fragmentation and support the scaling up of digital financial services across the Single Market. The EU Digital Finance Platform will initially consist of two main building blocks: an Observatory offering interactive features such as a FinTech Map, events and a section where users will be able to share relevant research material, and a Gateway which will act as a single access point to supervisors, with information about national innovation hubs, regulatory sandboxes and licensing requirements (European Commission, 2022[5]). This part of the Platform will also host functionalities linked to cross-border testing – a novelty enabling firms to involve multiple national authorities in the testing of new products or applications. In a second phase, to be launched in 2023, new features are set to be added to the EU Digital Finance Platform, building on user feedback (European Commission, 2022[5]).

3.1.1. Data and Open Finance

The European commission has been promoting several initiatives in recent years related to access and use of data, all being a part of its longer term strategy on data (European Commission, 2020[6]). The strategy aims at creating a single EU market for data, personal as well as non-personal data, including sensitive business data, where EU law can be enforced effectively, and where all data-driven products and services comply with the relevant norms of the EU's single market (European Commission, 2020[6]). Within the scope of this broad strategy, the European Commission has recently proposed two legislations – The Data Governance Act (European Commission, 2022[7]) and the Data Act (European Commission, 2022[8]). The first sets regulation on the re-use of publicly held, protected data and applies regulation to data intermediaries. Both personal and non-personal data are in scope of the Data Governance Act, and for personal data, the General Data Protection Regulation (GDPR) applies it also aims to facilitate the voluntary sharing of data by individuals and businesses. The second legislative initiative sets up rules on who can use and access what data and for which purposes.

More specific to financial data, in 2021, the Commission established an expert group on European financial data space to engage with stakeholders. A year later, a subgroup on open finance was created as open finance is considered to be an integral part of the European financial data space, along with data contained in public disclosures of firms as well as supervisory data (European Commission, 2022[9]). The access and reuse of customer data, with consent, across a range of financial services has already been referred to in the EU digital finance strategy.

Box 3.1. The EU Digital Finance Strategy

The Digital Finance Strategy adopted by the EU in 2020 sets out Europe's regulatory framework on the digital transformation of finance in the coming years, with emphasis on risks, data sharing and level playing field. The strategy sets out four main priorities: removing fragmentation in the Digital Single Market, adapting the EU regulatory framework to facilitate digital innovation, promoting a data-driven finance and addressing the challenges and risks with digital transformation, including enhancing the digital operational resilience of the financial system (European Commission, 2020[3]).

In May 2022, the Council presidency and the European Parliament reached a provisional agreement on the Digital Operational Resilience Act (DORA), one of the components of the Digital Finance Strategy, focused on harmonizing and improving the management of Information, Communication and Technologies (ICT) risks at financial institutions and critical ICT third-party service providers. DORA is expected to order the enactment of a financial services digital operational resilience act that will set consistent rules addressing the digital operational resilience needs of all regulated financial entities and establishing an oversight framework for critical ICT third-party providers. The regulation will cover a range of financial entities regulated at EU level, namely credit institutions, payment institutions, electronic money institutions, investment firms, crypto-asset service providers, central securities depositories, central counterparties, trading venues, trade repositories, managers of alternative investment funds and management companies, data reporting service providers, insurance and reinsurance undertakings, insurance intermediaries, reinsurance intermediaries and ancillary insurance intermediaries, institutions for occupational retirement pensions, credit rating agencies, statutory auditors and audit firms, administrators of critical benchmarks and crowdfunding service providers (European Commission, 2022[10]). The one-off costs associated with the proposal are mainly due to investments in IT systems. For large financial firms, implementing the measures are likely to be low due to previous investment. For smaller firms, the costs are expected to be low as well, as they would be subject to less stringent measures proportionate to their lower risk (European Commission, 2022[10]). However, given the CNB dissatisfaction with the level of applications for payment service provider licenses, the additional requirements set in the DORA regulation might negatively affect the already lengthy process of authorisation in this sector.

Revision of Payment Services Directive 2 (PSD2)

Sections 1.2 and 4.2 point to the fact that many Czech FinTechs operate in fields related to Payment services and that access to data provided by standardised APIs are a valuable component of their business. Thus, the PSD2 regulation and the open banking framework that it introduced are a significant component of the FinTech industry in the Czech Republic. Hence, it is expected that the revision of PSD2 currently underway at the European commission and the open finance framework that is being promoted will have a substantial effect on local FinTechs and their prospect of growth. The European Commission launched in May 2022 a Public Consultation on the Review of the Revised Payment Services Directive (PSD2) (European Commission, 2022[11]). This consultation was addressed to the general public and to a broad range of stakeholders and aims to report on the application and impact of EU rules on payment services and to assess whether PSD2 application remains fit for purpose. Such revision is closely interlinked with the open finance initiative, and according to the Consultation, lessons learned from PSD2 as regards third-party service providers' access rights to payment accounts upon customer request will be taken into account when designing the open finance framework. The Commission has an ambition to propose legislation on a broader open finance framework which would allow for customers' data to be shared beyond the scope of PSD2 provided that there is a customer agreement as well as the effective application of data protection rules and security safeguards (European Commission, 2022[11]).

A separate targeted consultation on Open Finance framework and Data Sharing in the financial sector was launched in May 2022 (European Commission, 2022[9]). As opposed to the general public consultation, this targeted consultation aimed to gather input from more professional stakeholders (such as individuals and organisations e.g. interest groups, member associations, and representative bodies that have more in-depth knowledge and/or (working) experience in the field of payments, such as PSPs, national- and EU authorities and – regulators, payment experts, etc.). However, the objectives of both consultations are the same.

Given the large proportion of Czech FinTechs operating in fields related to Payment Services, access to data provided by standardised APIs is a valuable component of their business model. Thus, the PSD2 regulation and the Open Banking framework that it introduced are a significant component underling the FinTech industry in the Czech Republic. Hence, it is expected that the revision of PSD2 currently underway, and the Open Finance framework that is proposed, will have a substantial effect on local FinTechs and their prospect of growth.

The European Single Access Point (ESAP)

In November 2021 the Commission also adopted a Capital markets union package which among other things announced a legislative proposal on the European Single Access Point (ESAP) or initiatives regarding new open finance framework. ESAP will be a common source of public, free information about EU companies and investment products and will be established by the European Securities and Markets Authority (ESMA) and should become operational from 2024. Apart from financial data ESAP should also provide sustainable-related information and product data and by that enable better digital use and re-use of information and tackle national data-related fragmentation (European Commission, 2021[12]).

The Capital market union package also suggests that the new 'open finance' framework beyond the scope of the PSD2 will be based on the principle of a level playing field for existing and new entrants. The Commission will work with stakeholders and recently established expert group on a European financial data space on a first set of specific use cases (European Commission, 2021[12]). This effort should later result in a legislative proposal for a new open finance framework, building on and in full alignment with broader data access initiatives. The Commission will furthermore adopt a supervisory data strategy to enable EU financial supervisors to efficiently collect and effectively use the data they need to perform their tasks and to minimise the cost and burden for reporting entities." (European Commission, 2021[12]).

3.1.2. Regulation of markets in Crypto Assets (MiCA) and the DLT pilot regime

The 'Regulation on Markets in Crypto Assets' (MiCA) intends to boost innovation while preserving financial stability and protecting investors from risks related to crypto-assets (European Commission, 2022[13]). This regulation offers legal clarity and certainty for crypto-asset issuers and providers and will create a single licensing regime across all member states. The framework is expected to bring such assets providers into the financial regulation perimeter in the Czech Republic for the first time. It is to be expected that such entities will become subject to authorisation and supervision by the CNB, after local legislation will be put in place.

The rules allow operators authorised in one Member State to provide their services across the EU ("passporting"). Safeguards include capital requirements, custody of assets, a mandatory complaint holder procedure available to investors, and rights of the investor against the issuer. Issuers of significant asset-backed crypto-assets (so-called global 'stablecoins') would be subject to more stringent requirements (e.g. in terms of capital, investor rights and supervision) (European Commission, 2022[13]).

The Commission also proposes a distributed ledger technology (DLT) pilot regime for market infrastructures that wish to try to trade and settle transactions in financial instruments in crypto-asset form. The DLT pilot regime represents a so-called 'sandbox' approach – or controlled environment – which allows temporary derogations from existing rules so that regulators can gain experience on the use of DLT in market infrastructures, while ensuring that they can deal with risks to investor protection, market integrity and financial stability. The intention is to allow companies to test and learn more about how existing rules fare in practice (European Commission, 2022[13]).

A parallel effort on the side of the EU around the use of crypto-assets as a payment transfers venue, is the proposal to amend Regulation (EU) 2015/847 of the European Parliament and the Council of 20 May 2015 on information accompanying transfers of funds, extending to crypto assets the information requirements currently applying to wire transfers (European Comission, 2022[14]). These information sharing duties already apply to wire transfers through Regulation (EU) 2015/847 and are often referred to internationally as the "travel rule". This present amendment proposal aims at introducing in EU law requirements suggested by FATF to align the regime of transparency for payments services providers for transfer of funds to Virtual Asset Service Providers (VASPs). The amendment will oblige these actors – VASPs – to collect and make accessible data concerning the originators and beneficiaries of the transfers of virtual or crypto assets they operate (European Comission, 2022[14]). Though the Czech Republic already requires a wide range of service providers in crypto assets to be registered, it does not supervise them on an ongoing basis, in particular, the payment providers' regime does not apply. Thus the implementation of this proposed amendment will require significant adjustments, as in other EU countries. According to the impact assessment of the European Commission, the easiest option for application would be to modify the transfer of funds regulation to also encompass transfers of virtual assets. The implementation of the "travel rule" will introduce new specific requirements for both the newly-covered VASPs and those already covered in AMLD, requiring them to obtain, hold and share required and accurate information on virtual asset transfers users and make it available on request to appropriate authorities (European Comission, 2022[14]). Thus, a more ongoing framework of supervision will perhaps be called for, which could be entrusted to the Financial Analytical Office (FAÚ) or the CNB.

3.1.3. Artificial Intelligence (AI) Act Proposal

In 2021, The European Commission came forward with a proposal for the AI Act, a regulatory framework on AI systems. The chosen design of the framework is to set up regulatory harmonised rules predominantly for high-risk AI systems, with the possibility for all providers of non-high-risk AI systems to follow a code of conduct. The requirements will concern data, documentation and traceability, provision of information and transparency, human oversight and robustness and accuracy and would be mandatory for high-risk AI systems. The proposed rules will be enforced through a governance system at Member States level, building on already existing structures, and a co-operation mechanism at Union level with the establishment of a European Artificial Intelligence Board. With regard to financial services, AI systems intended to be used to evaluate the creditworthiness of consumers or establish their credit score, with the exception of AI systems put into service by small scale providers for their own use are regarded under the current proposal as high risk AI systems. The Commission may expand the list of high-risk AI systems used within certain pre-defined areas, by applying a set of criteria and risk assessment methodology (European Commission, 2021[15]). Thus, the direct effect on conduct of regulation and supervision in the sector of consumer credit is expected to be substantial, and indeed CNB official have assessed the expected impact of this regulation to be important.

3.1.4. Regulatory sandboxes in the EU

European Union supports the establishment of regulatory sandboxes throughout EU and considers them to be tools for an innovation-friendly, future-proof and resilient regulatory framework that masters disruptive challenges in the digital age. The benefits are seen mostly in the opportunity for innovation and growth for businesses, especially SMEs and businesses at a very early stage, and in promoting *proactive regulatory learning, enabling regulators to gain better regulatory knowledge and to find the best means to regulate innovations based on real-world evidence."* (European Union, 2020[16]). Apart from the financial regulatory sandboxes, EU supports them also in other fields such as AI or blockchain (European Union, 2020[16]). Further to this, the EU has published a call for tenders to contract a consortium, the mission of which would be to facilitate and operate a pan-European regulatory sandbox for DLT that would accompany the use cases developed on top of the European Blockchain Services Infrastructure (EBSI) (European Commission, 2022[17]).

According to the European Forum of Innovation facilitators (EFIF) as of August 2022 there were ten sandboxes operating in the EU/EEA namely in Austria, Denmark, Italy, Lithuania, Malta, the Netherlands, Norway, Poland, the Slovak Republic, and Spain (European Banking Authority, 2022[18]). Added to that list is a sandbox in Hungary operated by the Hungarian National Bank, Nemzeti Bank (Magyar Nemzeti Bank, 2022[19]). The European Forum for Innovation Facilitators is a platform for supervisors to engage with each other and share experiences and expertise on innovation facilitators. It is supposed to help co-ordinate views on the regulation and supervision of innovative financial services and products and to strengthen co-operation. Recently new initiative under the Digital finance platform appeared, specifically the cross-border testing framework, which enables the involvement of more than one national competent authority.

3.2. Czech industry associations and related industry initiatives

This section provides a brief overview of industry associations and initiatives of the FinTech sector in the Czech Republic, focusing on the work of associations and other networking activities.

3.2.1. The Czech FinTech Association

The Czech FinTech Association was established in 2016 and is with over 40 members as of September 2022[2] the biggest representative of Czech FinTech companies. The association´s role is to support innovation in the financial sector and represent the member´s views in dealing with the public or private sector. The association organises expert working groups, networking events, and aims to constitute a point of contact for innovators, investors, regulators, and business partners (Czech Fintech Association, 2020[20]).

3.2.2. The Technology Platform for Communication Tools and IoT (CTIT)

The CTIT was established with the aim of supporting the Czech organisations in the digital economy, with the main focus on FinTech and the digitalisation of the financial sector. They do so through conveying knowledge in the field by organizing conferences, lectures, publishing and collecting and compiling information and literature, by providing expert opinions and advice on digitalisation and FinTech and by providing information on funding opportunities. They also publish FinTech podcasts, overview of Czech FinTech companies or FinTech Roadmap (CTIT, 2022[21]).

3.2.3. FinTech Media and related initiatives

There are two main FinTech focused online media sources in the Czech Republic. FinTech Cowboys, an e-magazine that publishes FinTech news from home and abroad, tests the latest products and services, writes reviews, publishes interviews, and connects professionals (especially from start-ups and financial institutions) and the general public (FinTech Cowboys, 2022[22]) and Fintree.cz, also e-magazine that focuses on articles, reviews and tips from the world of FinTech (Fintree, 2022[23]) Fair Fintech is a group of young FinTech companies which created this initiative for the goal to cultivate the market and the industries in which they do business and to help their clients to avoid bad deals. They also offer "fairness audit" for other FinTech companies. This service provides the other FinTechs with an evaluation which confirms whether their service, product and/or terms and conditions are "fair" (Fér Fintech, 2022[24]).

3.2.4. FinTech Hub

The FinTech Hub was established in 2021 in the Slovak Republic by Mastercard and Vacuumlabs in co-operation with the Slovak FinTech Association. Since then, already 15 companies from the Slovak Republic, the Czech Republic, Hungary, Romania and Ukraine (all from CEE region) have joined. In April 2022 a branch office was established in the Czech Republic where Seed starter by Česká spořitelna and Czech FinTech Association joined as partners. FinTech Hub aims to increase the level of innovation and competitiveness of the digital market in the Czech Republic and Central Europe and for this purpose offers variety of services for the young firms, such as legal and other advice, mentoring, independent testing environments or connecting them with investors or other key partners (Fintech Hub, 2022[25]).

3.2.5. CzechInvest

CzechInvest is a state contributory organisation, business, and investment promotion agency, which is subordinate to the Ministry of Industry and Trade of the Czech Republic and has a combination of regional, central, and international operations. One of its activities is focused on start-ups. They offer broad scale of initiatives for start-ups, such as mentoring (technology, business strategy and marketing), consulting services, arranging participation in international conferences, providing mentors and offices for three months abroad, airfare reimbursement, brokering investments for both investors and start-ups with reaching out to domestic and foreign partners, customers and investors. Their ecosystem consists of hundreds of start-ups, but also top experts in the Czech Republic or abroad. According to the CzechInvest's annual report for 2021, 92 innovative companies were provided with incubation, mentoring, or assistance when expanding abroad last year through the programs CzechAccelerator, CzechDemo and CzechMatch (CzechInvest, 2021[26]).

3.3. Demand side and consumer adoption

This section provides a brief overview of the demand side in the Czech Republic, focusing on financial assets and credit to the non-financial private sector, level of financial literacy and digital skills of Czech consumers and their overall financial behaviour.

The savings rate within the Czech economy is relatively high, about 29% of gross national income (MFCR, 2019[27]). However, Czech households rank in the bottom of OECD countries with regard to overall financial assets held (Figure 3.1). More than half of households' savings are held in cash and deposits and only a tiny fraction of savings enters the capital market (MFCR, 2019[27]). This is mainly due to the very conservative investment outlook of Czech households, which has not fundamentally changed over the past decade and a half; the total portion of household assets placed in exchange-traded shares, debt securities and investment funds (i.e. traditional capital market products) was 12.3% in 2016 (MFCR, 2019[27]). In addition, compared to OECD countries, the Czech households have in particular low ratio of financial assets held through financial intermediaries (institutional investors) (Figure 3.2). These "intermediated assets" include investment fund shares, life insurance and annuity entitlements and pension entitlements. Indeed, Czech households have low amounts of assets accumulated in both pension funds and life insurance reserves due to low amounts of retirement savings flowing to defined contribution schemes (see Annex A).

Figure 3.1. Financial assets of households and NPISHs, 2020

Percentage of Net Disposable Income (NDI)

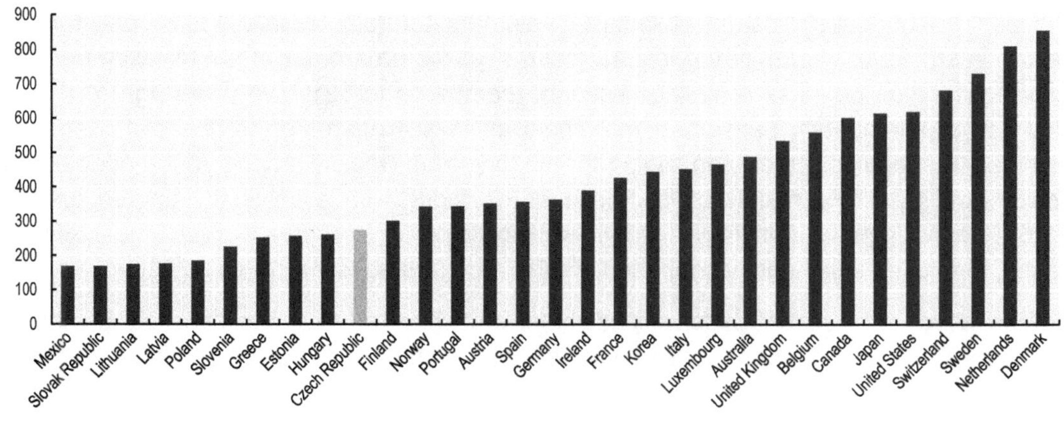

Source: OECD stat.

Figure 3.2. Financial assets indirectly held by households and NPISHs, 2020

Percentage of total financial assets

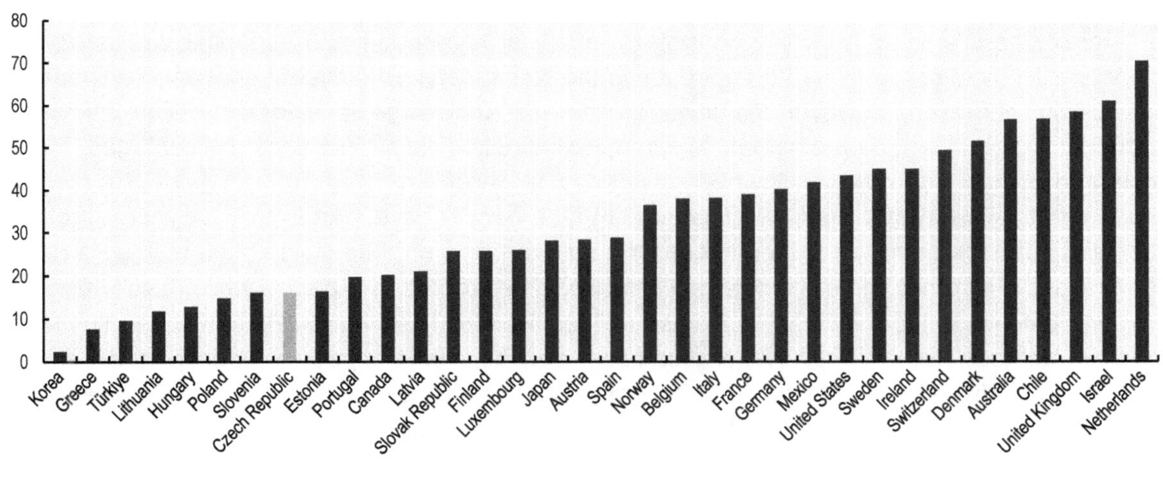

Source: OECD stat.

3.3.1. Financial literacy and financial behaviour of consumers

Financial education is the competence of the Ministry of Finance of the Czech Republic (MFCR) (see Section 2.1.1). The MFCR, based on discussion with the Working group on financial education, published in 2020 a National Strategy on Financial Education which sets out the direction that financial education in the Czech Republic should take in the coming years (available in Czech) (MFCR, 2020[28]). Among other initiatives in this regard, the MFCR runs an informational website about financial literacy which provides a lot of useful tips for consumers, including a national registry maintenained by the MFCR of on-going financial education projects (MFCR, 2022[29]).

In 2020, the MFCR also conducted a survey on the level of financial literacy among adult citizens (MFCR, 2020[30]). The evaluation of the survey provided a very detailed insight into the level of financial awareness and financial literacy of retail consumers in the Czech Republic. For example, in the field of money management it showed that 69% of adults realise that it is a good idea to spread their investments over several places. 10% of households use collective investment, up from 2% in 2015, but only 5% of people have invested in stocks or shares in the last 12 months. In the area of saving, it for example concluded that 56% of households now use a savings account (compared to 32% five years ago) or that 51% of households use supplementary pension or retirement savings. Regarding the financial mindset 28% of people admitted to spending rather than saving for the long term (mainly among young people under 30). The opposite view was held mainly by people over 60, those with a university degree and the self-employed. 64% of households (similarly to 2015) were building up a reserve in case of loss of income. In 31% of cases, they used a savings account and in 28% a current account (MFCR, 2020[30]).

The data of the survey showed that Czech citizens have long preferred saving to investing. Saving is mostly done through saving in bank account (three-quarters) or through building savings. Compared to 2015, the proportion of those who also saved in cash has increased significantly from 34% to 58%. Czech citizens were also starting to take a more proactive approach to their own finances compared to 2015. The proportion of those who have started saving (from 35% in 2015 to 69% in 2020), set a clear financial plan (from 39% in 2015 to 64% in 2020) or cut back on some of their spending (from 35% in 2015 to 62% in 2020) has jumped. However, saving still prevails over investing, Czech citizens hold 12% of their savings in the capital market (and a further 7% in pension products) and 51% of their financial savings in bank accounts (citizens in the 15 countries that joined the European Union before 2004 hold 14% of their savings in capital market investments and 30% of their financial savings in bank accounts) (MFCR, 2019[27]).

When compared to the results of the 2015 survey, the final conclusions of the 2020 survey showed that the level of financial literacy, which consists of financial knowledge and economic responsibility, has increased slightly over the five-year period since the last survey. The level of economic responsibility of citizens has increased, however the level of financial knowledge is stagnating. Czechs were also performing worse in simple mathematical examples (simple division, fractions, percentages, trinomials, simple and compound interest). However, a positive tendency emerged, for example, in a more active attitude of citizens towards their own finances. In fact, people have started to save more, set financial goals, and cut back on some of their spending, and two-thirds of households have built up a reserve in case of a loss of income. There has been an increase in the proportion of people who consult their relatives or experts before signing a contract or in case of financial difficulties, but only a fifth of people know what Annual Percentage Rate (APR) is. When it comes to pensions, 95% of people expect part of their pension to be funded by the state, and since 2015 the proportion of those with a more responsible alternative plan has increased – they also want to fund their pension from savings, a private pension plan or by earning extra income (MFCR, 2020[30]).

When it comes to crypto-assets, Czech consumers are a bit hesitant to invest in these assets. According to the market research agency STEMMARK, only 9% of Czechs have tried investing in crypto-assets. The research further provides more detail stating that the source of crypto-assets for Czechs are mainly (53%) cryptocurrency exchanges or cryptocurrency exchange offices, with cryptocurrency wallets (20%) and traditional stock exchanges or exchange offices (12%) also being used as alternatives. In any case, 93% of the money circulating in crypto-assets is for savings that Czechs willing to put at risk without any serious repercussions if the capital is lost. The most frequent amounts invested are up to approx. EUR 2 000 (CZK 50 000).[3] Perhaps due to the current downturn in the value of crypto-assets, trust in crypto-assets has declined: In 2021, 39% of people did not trust them, while in 2022 the scepticism is up to 47% (STEM/MARK, 2022[31]).

3.3.2. Digital skills

Digital solutions in financial sector are in general quite widespread amongst Czechs and the population has a high uptake of some FinTech solutions. For example, in 2020 97% of Czech were using online banking (to compare, it was 82% in 2018). The population in the Czech Republic holds a relatively high score in the use of online banking among EU countries (Figure 3.3). Even though electronic banking is a popular tool among Czechs, 42% of them do not believe that the digital banking can completely substitute meeting with the banker in person, out of which 10% exclude such claim absolutely. However, using cashless payment methods and online solutions is very popular among Czech consumers as 61% of them prefer to pay by card when shopping offline (meaning all forms of contactless payments such as via smart phones, smart watches, etc.), 79% of respondents use internet banking at least 2-3 times a month and 69% use mobile banking as often as every day. Across European countries, Czechs are among the heavy users of online shipping (Figure 3.4). It can be therefore concluded, that even though a significant number of Czechs don´t want to rely on digital solution completely and prefer human interaction is some aspects, the majority in general prefers to communicate with their banks remotely.

Figure 3.3. People who use internet banking 2021

Percentage of individuals aged (16-74)

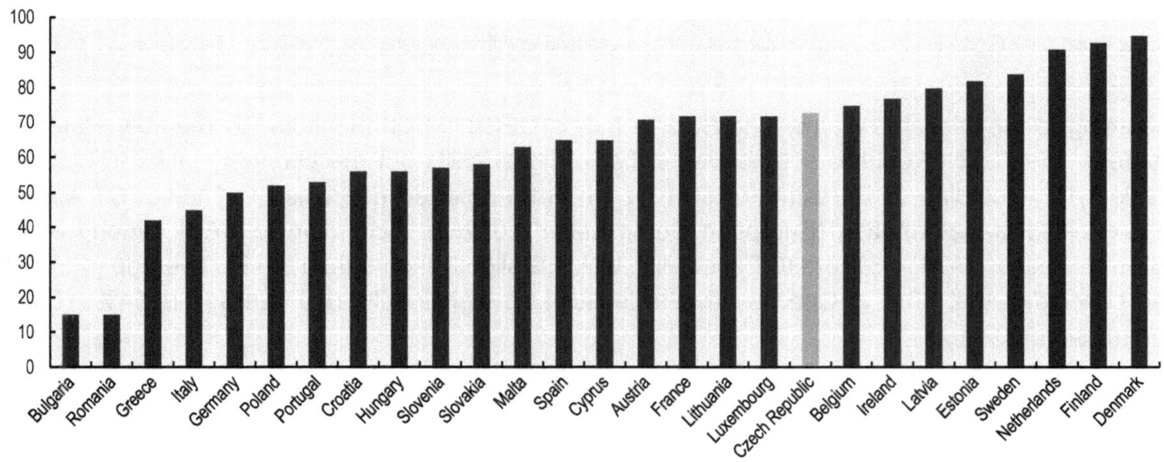

Source: Eurostat.

Figure 3.4. Use of mobile phone or internet for purchases, 2021

People (age 15+) who used a mobile phone or the internet to buy something online in the past year, in percentage

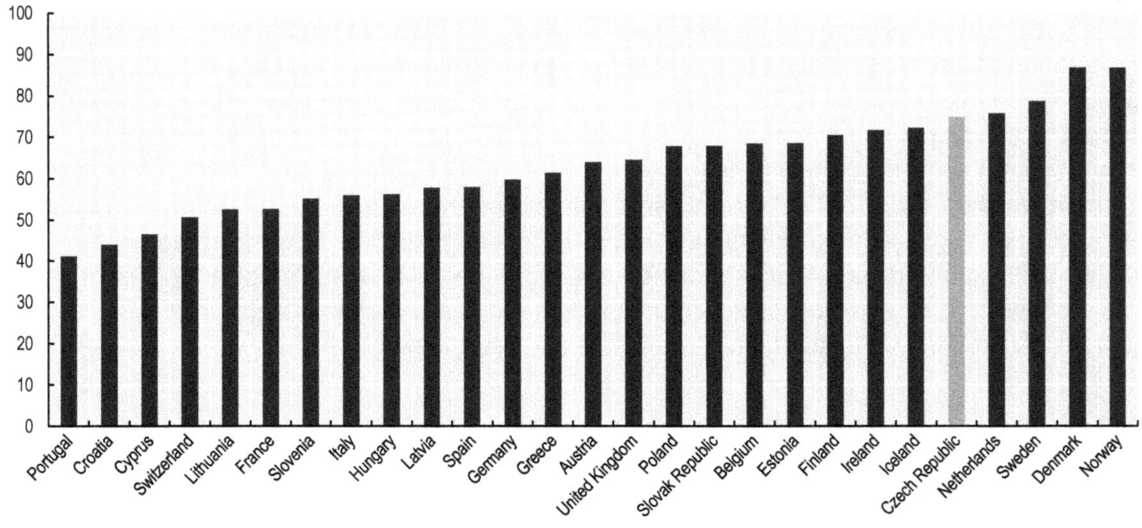

Source: World Bank Global Financial Inclusion database https://databank.worldbank.org/source/global-financial-inclusion

According to the Digital Economy and Society Index (DESI), which monitors EU member states' digital progress, the Czech Republic scores well in basic digital skills but the economy lacks ICT specialists (Table 3.1). According to Eurostat, 76% of Czech firms reported difficulties in finding ICT specialists, limiting digital transformation (European Commission, 2022[32]). According to DESI, among employed individuals aged 15-74, 4.6% are ICT specialist, which is slightly higher than the EU average (4.5%). DESI also concluded that 60% of Czechs have at least basic digital skills (EU average is 54%) (European Commission, 2022[32]).

Table 3.1. Digital economy and society indicators in the EU

	Czech Republic			Average EU / Top EU
	DESI 2020	DESI 2021	DESI 2022	DESI 2022
At least basic digital skills (% individuals)	NA	NA	60%	54% / 79%
ICT specialists (% individuals in employment aged 15-74)	4%	4%	5%	5% / 8%
Female ICT specialists (% ICT specialist)	10%	10%	10%	19% / 28%
SMEs with at least a basic level of digital intensity (% SMEs)	NA	NA	53%	55% / 86%
Big Data (% enterprises)	9%			14% (2020) / 31% (2020)
Artificial Intelligence (% enterprises)		4%		8% (2021) / 24% (2021)

Source: European Commission (2022[32]), Country Report-Czech Republic Accompanying the document Recommendation for a COUNCIL RECOMMENDATION on the 2022 National Reform Programme of the Czech Republic and delivering a Council opinion on the 20, https://eur-lex.europa.eu/legal-content/EN/ALL/?uri=CELEX%3A52022SC0605

3.4. Funding

3.4.1. Access to finance

Start-ups and young SMEs play a leading role in diffusing innovation in financial markets (by the introduction of new products, services or processes, new organisational methods or marketing techniques). Fostering innovation can raise productivity and spur economic growth.

There are well known barriers for innovation: access to finance, access to skilled human capital and access to networks (all along the supply chain – suppliers and clients). In particular, young Czech firms lack sufficient funding sources, in particular access to capital markets. There is also a little venture capital available (see Figure 3.5 reproduced below), which creates a finance gap for early-stage innovative firms. Bank credit is available but not always accessible for young start-ups without any previous financial history or finished product (OECD, 2020[33]). Access to finance is therefore difficult for young start-ups which can be seen also from the results of the questionnaire (see Chapter 4).

International Finance Organisations (European Investment Fund) have signed agreements with the Czech Government in order to stimulate growth-oriented firms seeking capital for their further development. Guarantees for SMEs and innovative projects are also provided by The Czech National Development Bank.

Because the financial system of the Czech Republic is bank-centric (see Annex A) and banks have a 74% share in the assets of the financial system the consequences are that the sources of financing of Czech companies are heavily dependent on (1) bank financing, (2) own resources and (3) subsidies from the European Union (in 2016, the value of loans amounted to 25.5% of corporate capital, listed shares 4.2% and bonds 3.6%). Most of the capital contributions of Czech companies come from the owners' own resources and reinvested profits, while most of the debt financing is obtained from banks. The share of financing through listed shares and bonds in Czech companies is half that of the EU average and one-third that of Germany or the UK (MFCR, 2019[34]).

Venture capital/private equity

In 2019 fundraising activities for start-ups in the Czech Republic in general generated almost EUR 100 m (CZK 2.54 bn)[4] and the volume of invested money increased by 127%, however a trend of growing investment activity of local funds and the weakening presence of the international ones can be noticed. Another trend that can be seen is the increased focus on financing small and medium-sized enterprises (Deloitte, 2020[35]).

Figure 3.5. Venture capital investment by country

Cumulative amounts for 2015-21, in m EUR

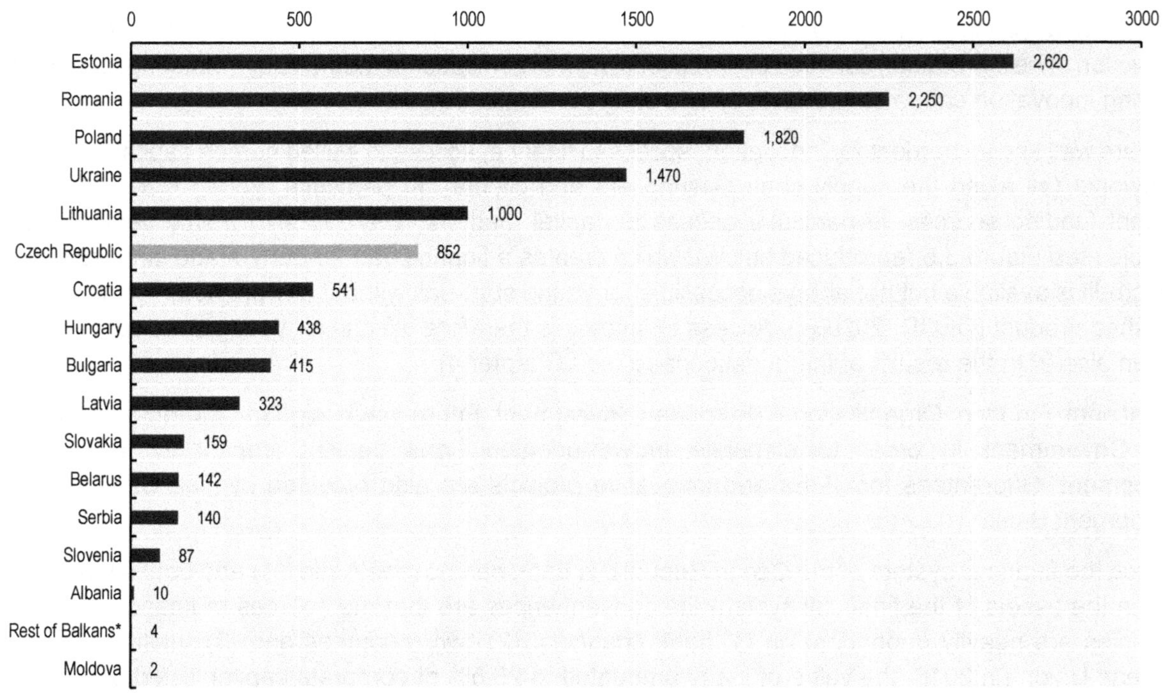

Note: (*) North Macedonia, Kosovo, Montenegro, Bosnia and Herzegovina.
Source: Google for Stratups, atomico and deealroom.co (2021[36]), Coming of age: Central and Eastern European startups, https://dealroom.co/reports/coming-of-age-central-and-eastern-european-startups

Figure 3.6. Venture capital funding per capita by country

Cumulative amounts for 2015-21, in EUR

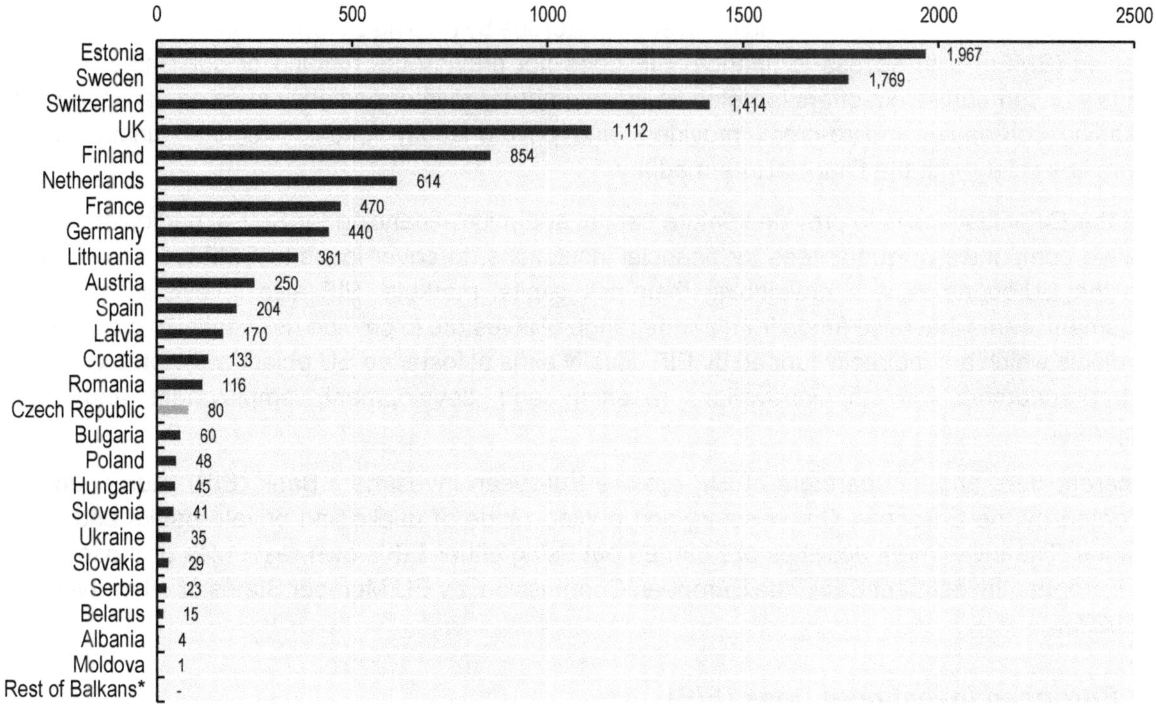

Note: *North Macedonia, Kosovo, Montenegro, Bosnia and Herzegovina.
Source: Google for Stratups, atomico and deealroom.co (2021[36]), Coming of age: Central and Eastern European startups, https://dealroom.co/reports/coming-of-age-central-and-eastern-european-startups

The Czech Private Equity and Venture Capital Association (CVCA)

CVCA is an association representing the interests of companies active in the area of private equity and venture capital in the Czech Republic. CVCA´s main objective is to promote and support private equity and venture capital and its development through, among other, elimination of administrative and legislative obstacles, and to increase awareness about the possibilities and importance of private equity and venture capital in the Czech Republic (CVCA, 2022[37]).

The Czech Business Angel Association (CBAA)

CBAA is the national association connecting angel investors in the Czech Republic and representing their interests. According to the Association, their aim is to build a vibrant investment climate that follows high professional standards and ethical principles. The main objective of CBAA is to nurture and promote active relations between investors and start-ups in the Czech Republic so that they provide a stable foundation for innovation and progress (CBAA, 2022[38]). In addition to networking across angel investors and start-ups, the association raises awareness of angel investing and represents the interests of investors at the national and international levels.

3.5. European funding support

3.5.1. European Investment Fund (EIF)

The EIF supports entrepreneurship and innovation in Europe by helping European small and medium sized companies (SMEs) with access to finance. EIF does not provide the funding or guarantees directly to individuals or companies but offers targeted financial products to intermediaries such as banks, guarantee and leasing companies, micro-credit providers and private equity funds. The final funding approval therefore lies solely with the financial intermediary.

One of the EIF initiatives is to provide venture capital and micro-financing for SMEs, particularly new and innovative companies or guarantees for financial institutions, to cover loans to SMEs. By that helps the EIF to the EU countries with developing their risk capital markets. EIF also invests in independent management teams that raise funds from a wide range of investors to provide risk capital to growing SMEs. The projects which are indirectly funded by EIF usually aims at fostering EU objectives, notably in the field of entrepreneurship, growth, innovation, research and development, employment and regional development.

The shareholders and key partners of EIF are the European Investment Bank (EIB), European Union, represented by the European Commission, and a wide range of public and private banks and financial institutions. The investment activities are carried out using either EIF's own resources or those provided by the European Investment Bank, the European Commission, by EU Member States or other third parties (EIF, 2022[39]).

3.5.2. European Investment Bank (EIB)

The EIB is the European Union's investment bank which funds projects that achieve the policy aims of the European Union by providing loans, guarantees and technical assistance. The focus of EIB is in areas such as climate, environment, small and medium sized enterprises (SMEs), development, cohesion and infrastructure. The loans provided by EIB are usually long-term loans that typically cover up to 50% of a project's overall cost. The investments flow through intermediated lending partners to both public and private sector (mostly SMEs) in order to support growth and jobs. The intermediaries can then provide local and targeted funds. Only loans exceeding the amount of EUR 25 m are invested directly. Apart from debt financing, project financing and equity financing EIB also provides advising and technical assistance.

The EIB is jointly owned by the EU Member States and raises money from international capital markets. No money comes from EU budget, but EIB borrows money on capital markets and lends it on favourable terms to projects that support EU objectives. As an independent body, the EIB takes its own borrowing and lending decisions. It co-operates with other EU institutions, especially the European Commission, the European Parliament, and the Council of the EU (EIB, 2022[40]).

References

CBAA (2022), *Czech Business Angel Association*, https://www.cbaa.cz/en/index.html (accessed on 5 August 2022). [38]

CTIT (2022), *About Association CTIT*, https://www.ctit.cz/en/ (accessed on 5 August 2022). [21]

CVCA (2022), *About Us – CVCA*, https://cvca.cz/en/about-us/ (accessed on 5 August 2022). [37]

Czech Fintech Association (2020), *Home | Czech Fintech Association*, https://czechfintech.cz/en/ (accessed on 5 August 2022). [20]

CzechInvest (2021), *Výroční zpráva 2021*, https://www.czechinvest.org/getattachment/339cfbfb-b8ca-4f99-b9da-4e3d0de88821/Vyrocni-zprava-2021 (accessed on 11 October 2022). [26]

Deloitte (2020), *CVCA Private Equity Report 2019*, https://www.focus-economics.com/countries/czech-republic/news/monetary-policy/cnb-delivers-larger-than-anticipated-rate-cut-in-may (accessed on 5 August 2022). [35]

EIB (2022), *European Investment Bank*, https://www.eib.org/en/index.htm (accessed on 26 August 2022). [40]

EIF (2022), *European Investment Fund*, https://www.eif.org/index.htm (accessed on 26 August 2022). [39]

European Banking Authority (2022), *Cross sectoral work*, https://www.eba.europa.eu/about-us/organisation/joint-committee/cross-sectoral-work (accessed on 5 August 2022). [18]

European Comission (2022), *Proposal for a REGULATION OF THE EUROPEAN PARLIAMENT AND OF THE COUNCIL on information accompanying transfers of funds and certain crypto-assets (recast)*, https://eur-lex.europa.eu/legal-content/EN/TXT/?uri=CELEX%3A52021PC0422 (accessed on 1 August 2022). [14]

European Commission (2022), *Consultation document - Public consultation on the review of the revised payment services Directive (PSD2) and on open finance*, EUROPEAN COMMISSION DIRECTORATE-GENERAL FOR FINANCIAL STABILITY, FINANCIAL SERVICES AND CAPITAL MARKETS UNION, https://ec.europa.eu/info/sites/default/files/business_economy_euro/banking_and_finance/documents/2022-psd2-review-open-finance-consultation-document_en.pdf (accessed on 10 May 2022). [11]

European Commission (2022), *Consultation document - Targeted consultation on open finance framework and data sharing in the financial sector*, EUROPEAN COMMISSION DIRECTORATE-GENERAL FOR FINANCIAL STABILITY, FINANCIAL SERVICES AND CAPITAL MARKETS UNION, https://ec.europa.eu/info/sites/default/files/business_economy_euro/banking_and_finance/documents/2022-open-finance-consultation-document_en.pdf (accessed on 10 May 2022). [9]

European Commission (2022), *Country Report-Czechia Accompanying the document Recommendation for a COUNCIL RECOMMENDATION on the 2022 National Reform Programme of Czechia and delivering a Council opinion on the 2022 Convergence Programme of Czechia*, https://eur-lex.europa.eu/legal-content/EN/ALL/?uri=CELEX%3A52022SC0605 (accessed on 29 August 2022). [32]

European Commission (2022), *EU Digital Finance Platform launch event*, https://ec.europa.eu/info/events/finance-220408-eu-digital-finance-platform-event-launch_en (accessed on 5 August 2022). [5]

European Commission (2022), *Homepage | EU Digital Finance Platform*, https://digital-finance-platform.ec.europa.eu/ (accessed on 5 August 2022). [4]

European Commission (2022), *Proposal for a REGULATION OF THE EUROPEAN PARLIAMENT AND OF THE COUNCIL on digital operational resilience for the financial sector and amending Regulations (EC) No 1060/2009, (EU) No 648/2012, (EU) No 600/2014 and (EU) No 909/2014*, https://eur-lex.europa.eu/legal-content/EN/TXT/?uri=CELEX%3A52020PC0595 (accessed on 1 August 2022). [10]

European Commission (2022), *Proposal for a REGULATION OF THE EUROPEAN PARLIAMENT AND OF THE COUNCIL on harmonised rules on fair access to and use of data (Data Act)*, https://eur-lex.europa.eu/legal-content/EN/TXT/?uri=COM%3A2022%3A68%3AFIN (accessed on 3 August 2022). [8]

European Commission (2022), *Proposal for a REGULATION OF THE EUROPEAN PARLIAMENT AND OF THE COUNCIL on Markets in Crypto-assets, and amending Directive (EU) 2019/1937*, https://eur-lex.europa.eu/legal-content/EN/TXT/?uri=CELEX%3A52020PC0593 (accessed on 1 August 2022). [13]

European Commission (2022), *REGULATION (EU) 2022/868 OF THE EUROPEAN PARLIAMENT AND OF THE COUNCIL of 30 May 2022 on European data governance and amending Regulation (EU) 2018/1724 (Data Governance Act)*, https://eur-lex.europa.eu/legal-content/EN/TXT/?uri=CELEX%3A32022R0868 (accessed on 3 August 2022). [7]

European Commission (2022), *Regulatory sandbox for blockchain and legal advice for EBSI production phase*, https://digital-strategy.ec.europa.eu/en/funding/regulatory-sandbox-blockchain-and-legal-advice-ebsi-production-phase (accessed on 24 October 2022). [17]

European Commission (2021), *COMMUNICATION FROM THE COMMISSION TO THE EUROPEAN PARLIAMENT, THE COUNCIL, THE EUROPEAN ECONOMIC AND SOCIAL COMMITTEE AND THE COMMITTEE OF THE REGIONS Capital Markets Union - Delivering one year after the Action Plan*, https://eur-lex.europa.eu/legal-content/EN/TXT/?uri=CELEX:52021DC0720 (accessed on 5 August 2022). [12]

European Commission (2021), *proposal for a REGULATION OF THE EUROPEAN PARLIAMENT AND OF THE COUNCIL LAYING DOWN HARMONISED RULES ON ARTIFICIAL INTELLIGENCE (ARTIFICIAL INTELLIGENCE ACT) AND AMENDING CERTAIN UNION LEGISLATIVE ACTS*, https://eur-lex.europa.eu/legal-content/EN/TXT/?uri=CELEX%3A52021PC0206 (accessed on 3 August 2022). [15]

European Commission (2020), *COMMUNICATION FROM THE COMMISSION TO THE EUROPEAN PARLIAMENT, THE COUNCIL, THE EUROPEAN ECONOMIC AND SOCIAL COMMITTEE AND THE COMMITTEE OF THE REGIONS A European strategy for data*, https://eur-lex.europa.eu/legal-content/EN/TXT/?uri=CELEX%3A52020DC0066 (accessed on 3 August 2022). [6]

European Commission (2020), *Digital finance package*, https://ec.europa.eu/info/publications/200924-digital-finance-proposals_en (accessed on 1 August 2022). [3]

European Commission (2018), *FinTech Action plan: For a more competitive and innovative European financial sector*, https://eur-lex.europa.eu/legal-content/EN/TXT/?uri=CELEX:52018DC0109 (accessed on 4 August 2022). [2]

European Union (2020), *Council Conclusions on Regulatory Sandboxes and Experimentation Clauses as tools for an innovation-friendly, future-proof and resilient regulatory framework that masters disruptive challenges in the digital age*, https://eur-lex.europa.eu/legal-content/EN/TXT/?uri=CELEX%3A52020XG1223%2801%29 (accessed on 5 August 2022). [16]

Fér Fintech (2022), *Fér Fintech | Férový a partnerský přístup v podnikání*, https://ferfintech.cz/ (accessed on 5 August 2022). [24]

FinTech Cowboys (2022), *FinTech Cowboys – Magazín o české fintech scéně.*, https://fintechcowboys.cz/ (accessed on 5 August 2022). [22]

Fintech Hub (2022), *Fintech Hub*, https://www.fintechhubeurope.com/ (accessed on 5 August 2022). [25]

Fintree (2022), *Fintree - Děláme FinTech dostupnější*, https://fintree.cz/ (accessed on 5 August 2022). [23]

Google for Stratups, atomico and deealroom.co (2021), *Coming of age: Central and Eastern European startups*, https://dealroom.co/reports/coming-of-age-central-and-eastern-european-startups (accessed on 23 August 2022). [36]

i5 invest (2022), *The 2022 European Unicorn & Soonicorn Report - European Tech Startups*, https://europeanunicornmap.com/ (accessed on 4 August 2022). [1]

Magyar Nemzeti Bank (2022), *REGULATORY SANDBOX*, https://www.mnb.hu/en/innovation-hub/regulatory-sandbox (accessed on 26 August 2022). [19]

MFCR (2022), *Finanční gramotnost aneb Proč se finančně vzdělávat?*, https://financnigramotnost.mfcr.cz/ (accessed on 5 August 2022). [29]

MFCR (2020), *FINANČNÍ GRAMOTNOST 2020*, https://financnigramotnost.mfcr.cz/cs/pro-odborniky/mereni-urovne-financni-gramotnosti/2020/vysledky-mereni-financni-gramotnosti-20-3286#vysledky (accessed on 5 August 2022). [30]

MFCR (2020), *Národní strategie finančního vzdělávání 2.0*, https://www.psfv.cz/cs/pro-odborniky/strategicke-dokumenty (accessed on 5 August 2022). [28]

MFCR (2019), *National Strategy for the Development of the Capital Market in the Czech Republic for the period of 2019-2023*, https://www.mfcr.cz/assets/en/media/201903-National-Strategy-CZ-Capital-Market.pdf (accessed on 1 July 2022). [27]

MFCR (2019), *National Strategy for the Development of the Capital Market in the Czech Republic for the period of 2019-2023*, https://www.mfcr.cz/assets/en/media/201903-National-Strategy-CZ-Capital-Market.pdf (accessed on 1 July 2022). [34]

OECD (2020), *OECD Economic Surveys: Czech Republic 2020*, OECD Publishing, Paris, https://doi.org/10.1787/1b180a5a-en. [33]

STEM/MARK (2022), *Přestože je nabídka kryptoměn stále pestřejší, důvěra v ně meziročně klesla*, https://www.stemmark.cz/prestoze-je-nabidka-kryptomen-stale-pestrejsi-duvera-v-ne-mezirocne-klesla/ (accessed on 5 August 2022). [31]

Notes

[1] Blockchain is a type of distributed ledger technology (DLT) that records transactions as a chain of blocks. For the purposes of this report, Blockchain and distributed ledger technologies (DLTs) are used interchangeably.

[2] Based on figures provided by the Czech FinTech Association.

[3] Based on exchange rate as of 31 December 2021 which was CZK 24.860 for EUR 1.

[4] Based on exchange rate as of 31 December 2019 which was CZK 25.41 for EUR 1.

4 OECD Questionnaire findings

This chapter presents the results of the OECD FinTech market questionnaire, which had an approximately 20% response rate (a quarter of the total FinTech sector). Results are likely to be skewed towards firms in their early stages or with pain points and can be interpreted as an upper bound on the hurdles the Czech FinTech face. The answers highlight the crucial role of data for financial innovation in the Czech Republic and the importance of inter-institutional collaboration between FinTechs, the regulator and financial intermediaries. Regulation is perceived as the key challenge, followed by access to market and funding. There is also a potential new risk to the system, such as the concentration on new dominant and unregulated payers.

In June 2022, the OECD launched an online open questionnaire on FinTech activity in the Czech Republic. Twenty-four FinTech companies (17 individual answers and 7 FinTechs operating under the aegis of FinTech Hub) provided detailed responses to this Questionnaire as of 5 October 2022, out of a total of c.100 Czech FinTech companies' universe. These companies are headquartered in the Czech Republic or in the Slovak Republic, and 42% of these FinTechs target only the Czech market (Figure 4.1).

In terms of geography of operations, more than half of the respondent FinTech headquarters are located in the Czech Republic, but equally, half of responding FinTechs have operations on a pan-European level (Figure 4.1). Passporting rights enable FinTech firms that are authorised in any EU or EEA state to freely trade in the Czech Republic (as in any other member state) following notification of the host authorities (see Section 4.1). These passports are the foundation of the EU single market for financial services. The possibility of foreign non-EU FinTech companies benefitting from a relatively lower regulatory burden and of prey firms establishing in the Czech market is a possible concern to Czech authorities, given potential risks to customer safety and investor protection.

Figure 4.1. Respondent Czech FinTech operation markets

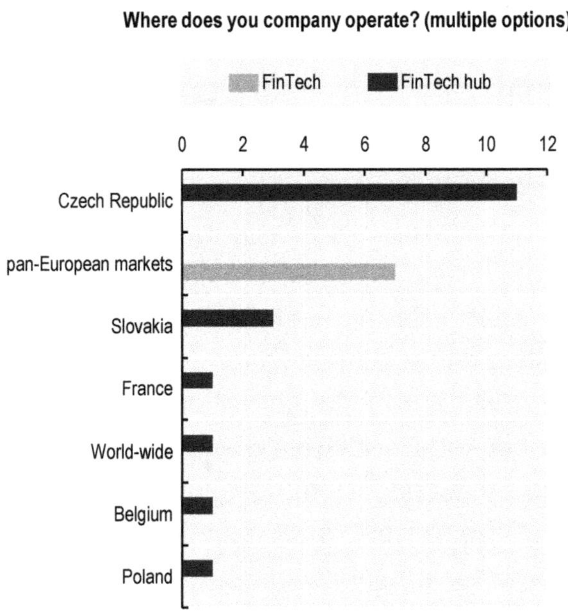

Source: Based on a sample of 24 responses (17 individual responses and 7 answers through FinTech Hub) by Czech FinTechs to the OECD Questionnaire.

The majority of firms that answered the questionnaire operate in the payments and electronic money services provision (Figure 4.2).

Figure 4.2. Czech FinTech sector of operation

Source: Based on a sample of 24 responses by Czech FinTechs to the OECD Questionnaire.

The majority of the firms responding to the questionnaire are in the seed stage of their lifecycle (Figure 4.3). Firms in the seed and early stages usually are the ones that benefit the most from the collaboration and interaction with industry mentors and government officials (World Bank, 2022[1]), in order to navigate regulatory requirements and to learn from veteran experiences.

Figure 4.3. Czech FinTech average growth stage, 2022

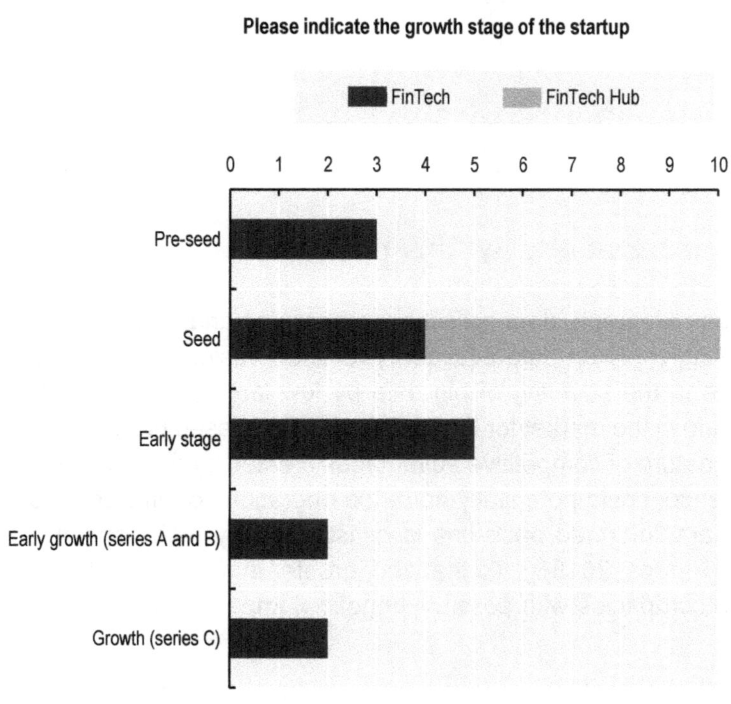

Source: Based on a sample of 24 responses by Czech FinTechs to the OECD Questionnaire.

4.1. Types of FinTech innovation in the OECD sample: the key role of data

Access to data is critical for FinTechs and data is at the core of most FinTech activity (e.g. artificial intelligence business models in trading; lending; blockchain-based uses in finance (OECD, 2021[2]). FinTechs are technology-native and combine the agility of start-ups with data processing and crunching abilities. Indeed, more than 60% of respondents to the OECD Questionnaire stated that access to both financial and non-financial data is beneficial to their business development. The two firms that answered that more data is not necessarily beneficial to their business development work in providing security solutions to digital applications and on online invoicing (Figure 4.4).

Figure 4.4. Czech FinTech perceptions on data availability, 2022

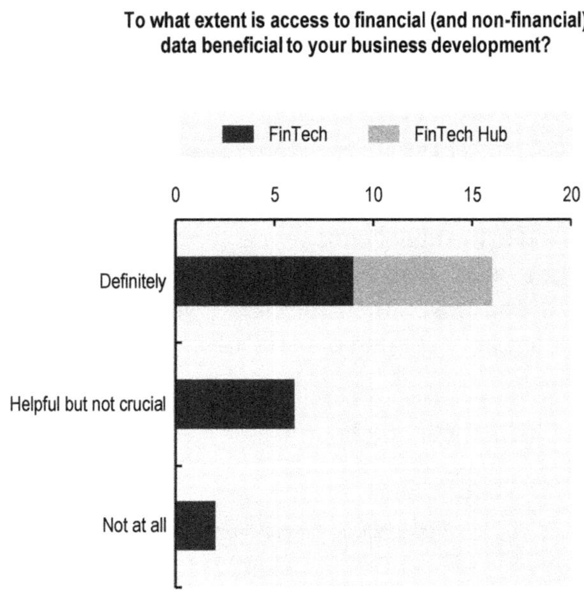

Source: Based on a sample of 24 responses by Czech FinTechs to the OECD Questionnaire.

4.2. Reported data accessibility by Czech FinTechs

As stated in the previous paragraph, data collection, processing and analytics play a key role in FinTech innovations that increasingly rely on data availability for their business models. Unequal access to data and potential dominance in the sourcing of big data by few large players could reduce the capacity of smaller players to compete in the market for FinTech innovation-based products/services (OECD, 2021[2]). In fact, the strength and nature of competitive advantages created by advances in innovative technologies such as artificial intelligence, could potentially harm the operations of efficient and competitive markets if consumers' ability to make informed decisions is constrained by high concentrations amongst market providers (Mnuchin and Phillips, 2018[3]). To that end, greater availability of data can be conducive to the development of start-up companies with possible beneficial impact on competitive conditions in financial markets.

The OECD survey shows that most innovations used by respondent Czech FinTechs evolve around data, data sharing and data usage for the development of products and services. In particular, 88% of firms use APIs to access data, more than half of respondent firms use big data and 63% of firms use cloud computing – all evolving around data at the core of their business model. Other digital technologies used include distributed ledger technologies (DLTs) (33% of respondents) and digital ID services (25% of respondent firms) (Figure 4.5).

Figure 4.5. Czech FinTech types of innovation used

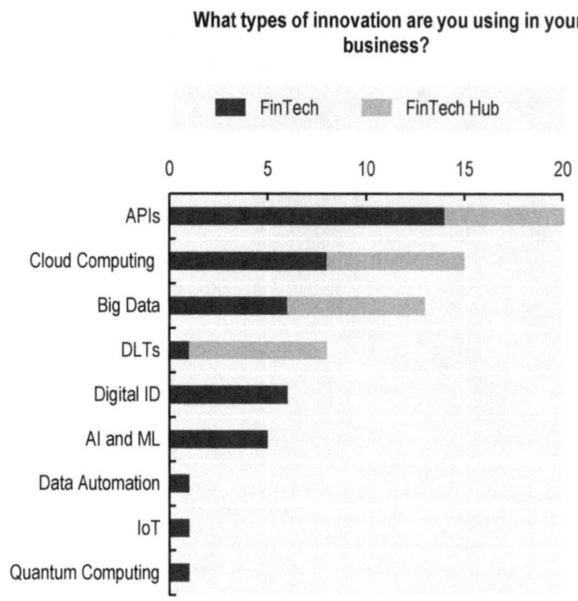

Source: Based on a sample of 24 responses by Czech FinTechs to the OECD Questionnaire.

Incumbent firms usually have costly legacy and potentially obsolete infrastructure and rather inefficient processes associated to such infrastructure, which, combined with cultural reluctance for change may prevent or slow down in-house FinTech innovation. The definition of what a bank is, is being called into question. Moreover, the speed of adoption of digital technologies and FinTech products and services by customers, and the marked acceleration in the demand for such products, particularly since the COVID-19 pandemic, is driving incumbent co-operation with FinTechs.

Access to data is one part of the needs of FinTechs that can be satisfied by such co-operation with incumbent financial institutions. As many start-ups are in the seed stage (Figure 4.3), they can benefit from monetary investment and expertise from co-operation with incumbents or investment by incumbents in their capital. This expertise comes from the knowledge of the business and the ecosystem, and the network effects add to the possible upside of such co-operation.

As FinTechs operate with third-party data, interdependences are created with data and digital service providers that might pose new risks to the system, such as the concentration on new dominant unregulated players. BigTechs, for example, increasingly leverage their free access to vast amounts of customer data that feed into artificial intelligence-driven models to provide financial services, their deployment of AI raises issues around data privacy and concerns over ways in which the collection, storage and use of personal data may be exploited for commercial gain. These practices could disadvantage customers, such as through discriminatory practices related to credit availability and pricing (OECD, 2021[2]).

The vast majority of respondents to the questionnaire highlighted the importance of accessing financial data for their business (88%), and more than 50% highlighted the need to access personal data, which serves for the personalisation of products and services, along with non-financial data (55%), potentially spurring the financial inclusion of underbanked customers (Figure 4.6).

APIs are the most frequent form of tool allowing for data accessibility by FinTechs (88%), along with aggregators and special purchases from specialised firms (58%). Screen scraping (own data production) is also a frequent form of data gathering, used by 42% of respondents to the questionnaire (RHS of Figure 4.6).

Figure 4.6. Czech FinTech data needs, 2022

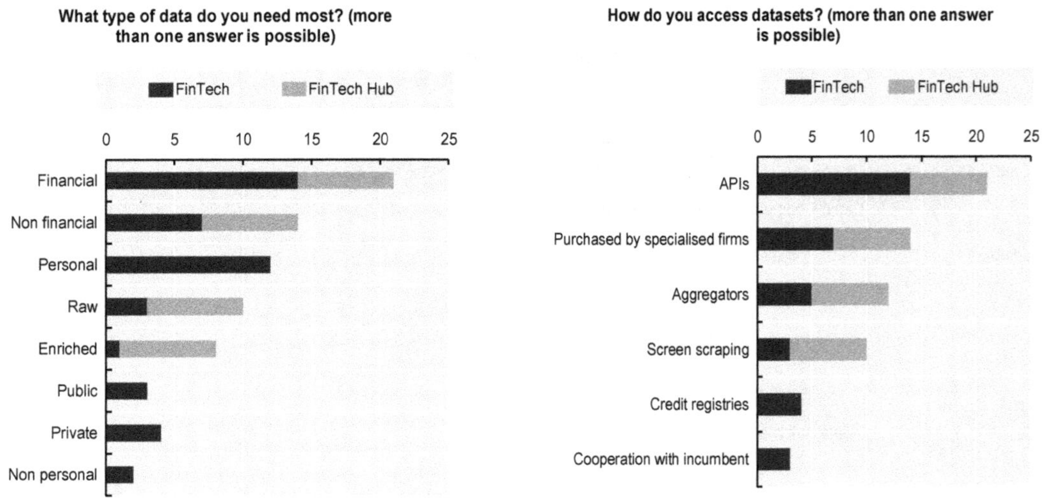

Source: Based on a sample of 24 responses by Czech FinTechs to the OECD Questionnaire.

When it comes to FinTechs sharing their own data, 83% of respondents reported that they do not share data beyond what is required by law, for different reasons. For larger firms, data is part of their key inputs; for early-stage firms, data is not part of their monetisation case yet.

Even when it comes to data sharing secured by formal regulatory arrangements and frameworks, data accessibility is not guaranteed. More than 46% of firms responding to the OECD Questionnaire have had problems accessing customer data from financial intermediaries. There are technical and strategic reasons explaining the problems: respondents reported that external APIs do not function properly in many cases, while others claimed that banks should be required by law to digitally sign documents.

There is a role for policy makers to reduce barriers to market entry by limiting abusive dominant practices that impede competition and create risks of market concentration with detrimental impact on financial consumers, as well as systemic risk. At a minimum, existing frameworks for data sharing arrangements should be promoted and their correct implementation safeguarded.

4.3. Reported hurdles to FinTech innovation in the Czech Republic

Financial regulation existing across the board for financial services safeguards market integrity, consumer protection and promotes financial stability (OECD, 2021[2]). From the industry standpoint, it provides for legal certainty that allows companies with innovative business models to develop and grow. At the same time, regulatory compliance is usually perceived by young start-up firms as a hurdle, given the associated cost and time commitment (World Bank, 2022[1]; OECD, 2020[4]) although it is unanimously agreed that regulation is essential to keep customers safe and to preserve the stability of the system. According to the findings of the OECD questionnaire, the most important reported hurdles to FinTech innovations in the Czech Republic are related to regulation: lack of regulatory clarity (67%), red tape (63%), licensing and supervisory requirements (58%), followed by entry barriers (54% of respondents) (Figure 4.7). Procedures for starting a business are more burdensome and time consuming than in most other OECD economies and the Czech Republic ranks 134th in the 2020 Doing Business survey for the "starting a business" indicator (World Bank, 2020[5]). According to the OECD 2020 Czech Survey, resolving commercial disputes ("enforcing contracts") takes longer than on average in the OECD, and is more costly to businesses (OECD, 2020[4]).

Figure 4.7. Czech FinTech challenges, 2022

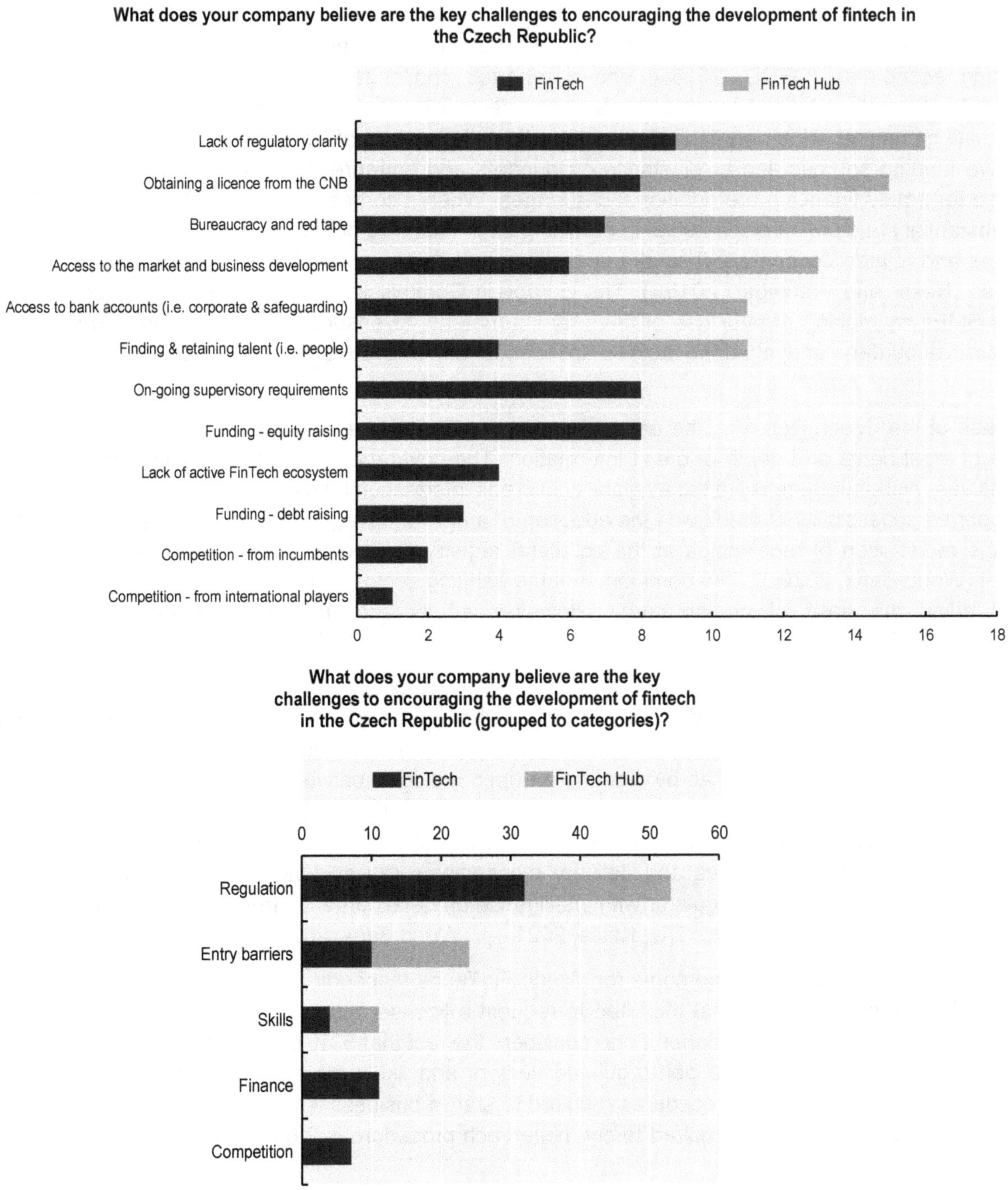

Source: Based on a sample of 24 responses by Czech FinTechs to the OECD Questionnaire. More than one answer is possible.

For 11% of the respondents, finding a retaining talent seems to be a concern, and could be related to the fact that these companies employ innovative technologies and mechanisms that require specialised skillsets by highly skilled employees. Nevertheless, when it comes to digitalisation skills, the Czech Republic is clustered in the group of OECD countries characterised by the highest skills proficiency (OECD, 2020[4]; Citibank, 2022[6]). On the other hand, in 2020, the European Commission suggested in its country report that although the Czech authorities are committed to the development and integration of new digital technologies, such effort is hampered by persistently low skills levels. For example, the Czech Republic still lags behind frontier Member States in terms of research and patent activities in this area (European Commission, 2020[7]).

Access to funding is one of the most commonly impediments to entrepreneurship across many OECD and developing economies (OECD, 2015[8]) and a reported challenge to Czech FinTech development (Figure 4.7). Overall, SMEs financing gaps may stem from an overreliance on the bank credit intermediation channel, which may be constraint particularly in times of stress. Lack of awareness about alternative funding sources and a reluctance of founders and entrepreneurs to relinquish ownership in exchange for equity financing are additional challenges. When it comes to market debt financing, SMEs have substantial structural disadvantages in obtaining such financing compared to large corporates given deal sizes and related economics of small transactions and disproportionate costs associated with such issuances (Nassr and Wehinger, 2015[9]). The European Commission has also recommended support towards SMEs by making greater use of financial instruments to ensure liquidity support, reducing the administrative burden, and ensuring access to finance for innovative firms (European Commission, 2020[7]).

In the case of the Czech Republic, the ease of getting credit is above the regional average and reflects strength of legal rights and depth of credit information. The coverage of credit information by the credit bureau is very high, but there is limited availability of credit information by credit registries. A recent action that supported accessibility of credit was the adoption of a new legal regime on secured transactions that allows the registration of receivables at the collateral registry and permits out-of-court enforcement of collateral (World Bank, 2020[5]). The dominance of the banking sector in the Czech financial system may also underline the ease of getting credit. However, equity and non-bank debt markets remain underdeveloped (see Section 5.1.3) and may hinder the development of FinTechs and the entire start-up ecosystem.

FinTech respondents signal as additional challenges the issues of access to market and business development. Regulatory sandboxes are one of the policy tools used to assist companies in overcoming the challenges on market access, as by creating an open dialogue between the regulator and the firm, they provide agility to the supervisory and regulatory framework ((World Bank, 2020[10]) (World Bank, 2020[11])). Indeed, regulatory sandboxes are beneficial to both parties: they allow innovators to test on a small scale their products, services and delivery mechanisms (as evidenced by the United Kingdom experience), while providing the regulator with intelligence on developments, trends and emerging risks ((Bromberg, Godwin and Ramsay, 2017[12]; Kalifa, 2021[13]), (World Bank, 2020[10]), (World Bank, 2020[11])).

Licensing also appears to be cumbersome for Czech FinTechs responding to the OECD Questionnaire: 40% of FinTech firms answered that they had to request a license more than once before successfully acquiring one. This figure is even higher if one considers the fact that 53% of the FinTechs responding to the Questionnaire are operating in non-regulated sectors and likely represent part of the "No" in this question. Indeed, the number of procedures required to start a business is twice as many as on average in OECD countries and the time required to complete each procedure is 2.6 times greater than the peer group (OECD, 2020[4]).

The reported cumbersome licensing process adds to FinTechs' perception of regulatory burden described above. There may be a need to clarify processes for licensing and authorisation and/or to educate new market entrants around applicable regulatory frameworks, particularly in areas of FinTech innovation, in order to address some of the reported impediments to FinTech development. It could also be noted that, interestingly, most Czech FinTechs operate in non-regulated sectors; the perceived burden of regulation evidenced by the OECD Questionnaire could perhaps further incentivise FinTechs to develop activity in non-regulated sectors so as to avoid such burden.

Figure 4.8. Czech FinTech dealing with supervision, 2022

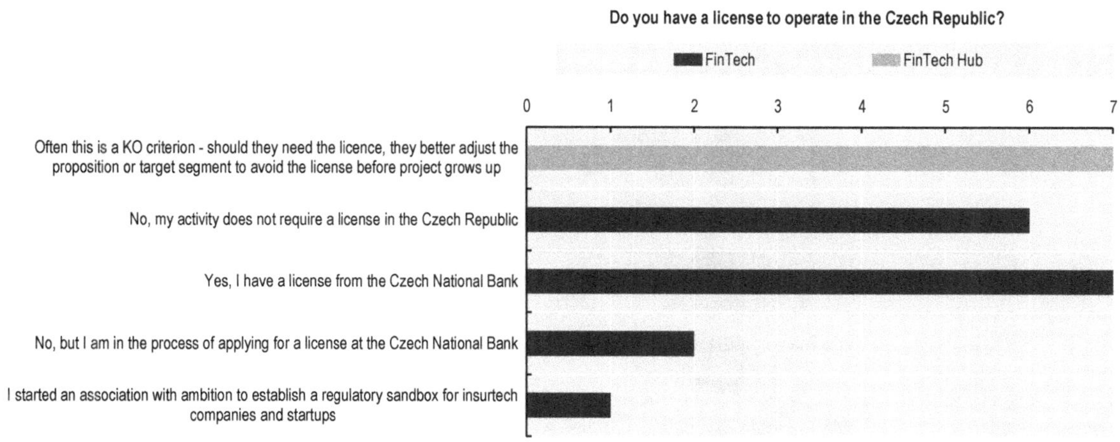

Source: Based on a sample of 24 responses by Czech FinTechs to the OECD Questionnaire.

The complex administrative procedure of establishment was also identified as one of the main obstacles for start-ups in the Czech Republic by the European Commission (European Commission, 2022[14]). Together with fast-changing legislation, complex administrative procedures are seen by the business sector as obstacles to investment, while the administrative burden is particularly problematic for start-ups in terms of licences and permits (European Commission, 2020[7]). The Commission therefore recommended that Czech Authorities remove the barriers hampering the development of a fully functioning innovation ecosystem (European Commission, 2019[15]).

4.4. FinTech perceptions on funding options in the Czech Republic

As mentioned above, access to finance constitutes one of the challenges for FinTech companies in the Czech Republic. Based on the responses to the OECD Questionnaire, the main investment source for Czech FinTechs is personal resources (37% of respondents), which is consistent with start-up and SME companies deploying own funds and friends and family financing (Berger and Udell, 2003[16]). Czech entrepreneurs rely mainly on their own resources and seed capital (68% of companies secured seed capital from own sources while only 48% were able to find an investor in a recent industry survey) (Deloitte Česká Republika, 2022[17]). In particular, 14% of start-ups raised initial funding from family or relatives and friends, while 5% took a loan from a bank. The overall difficulty of finding an investor was assessed in that survey as 5.33 on a scale from 1-10.

Domestic Venture Capital (VC) funding appears to be the second most important funding source in the group of respondents (18%). When combined with international VCs, this source of funding becomes the most widely used in the group (33% combined VC). These responses reflect the increase in VC activity by domestic funds in the Czech Republic although there is still room to develop further VC funding in the country relative to the levels observed in the rest of Europe (see Section 4.4). Czech FinTechs are also looking for VC as their main investment source in the future (Figure 4.9).

It should be also noted that none of the FinTech firms responding to the OECD Questionnaire received funding from the public sector (local or national) (Figure 4.9).

Figure 4.9. Czech FinTech access to finance, 2022

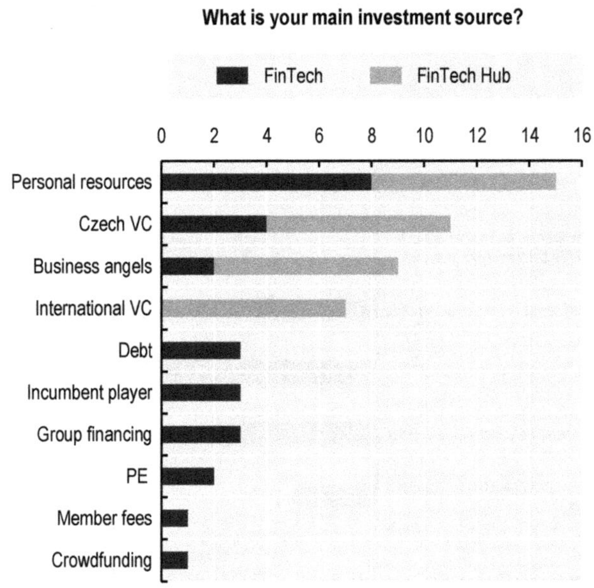

Source: Based on a sample of 24 responses by Czech FinTechs to the OECD Questionnaire.

The majority of respondents have a neutral or favourable opinion of the Czech Republic as an easy place to raise investment (Figure 4.10). A caution note can be made on this assertion, as only FinTechs who have successfully raised funding for their innovation have answered the OECD Questionnaire, so there is a possible survival bias and sample selection bias in this exercise (Keogh and Johnson, 2021[18]).

Figure 4.10. Czech FinTech expected funding sources, 2022

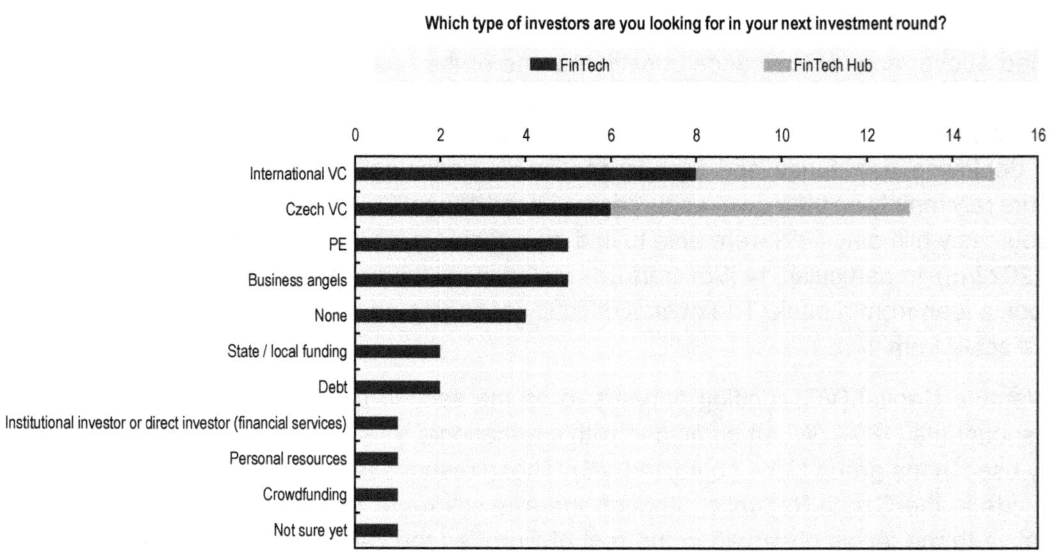

Source: Based on a sample of 24 responses by Czech FinTechs to the OECD Questionnaire.

Another interesting observation of the responses to the OECD Questionnaire relates to the exit strategy of responding FinTechs: the majority of FinTechs report to be in the business in order to be acquired by incumbents or larger FinTechs/BigTechs (M&A accounting for more than 64% of the responses). Although this is understandable, it is not conducive to increased competition in the market for financial services and are subject to the terms of the acquisitions (Figure 4.11).

Figure 4.11. Czech FinTech expected exit strategy, 2022

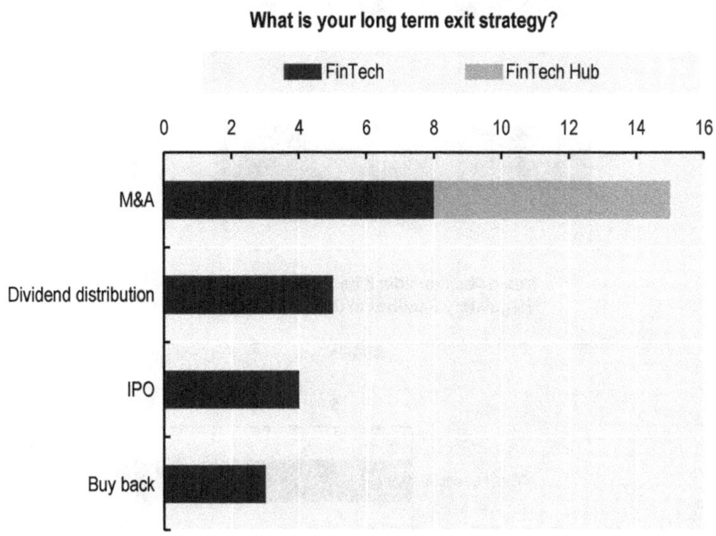

Source: Based on a sample of 24 responses by Czech FinTechs to the OECD Questionnaire.

4.5. Perceived benefit of a regulatory sandbox and focus on data

More than 77% of respondents to the OECD Questionnaire believe that it would be beneficial to introduce a regulatory sandbox in the Czech Republic.

According to the OECD survey, 71% of respondent FinTechs would be interested in a sandbox with a focus on data, if it was to become available (Figure 4.12). Two-thirds of these would only be interested depending on the terms of such sandbox. This highlights the importance of a well-thought design and structure of any future sandbox arrangement. It also highlights a possible lack of clear understanding of what a sandbox involves from the FinTech side. This underscores the importance of – clear communication and the required educational effort that may need to be undertaken in such effort.

Figure 4.12. Perceived interest in a data sandbox

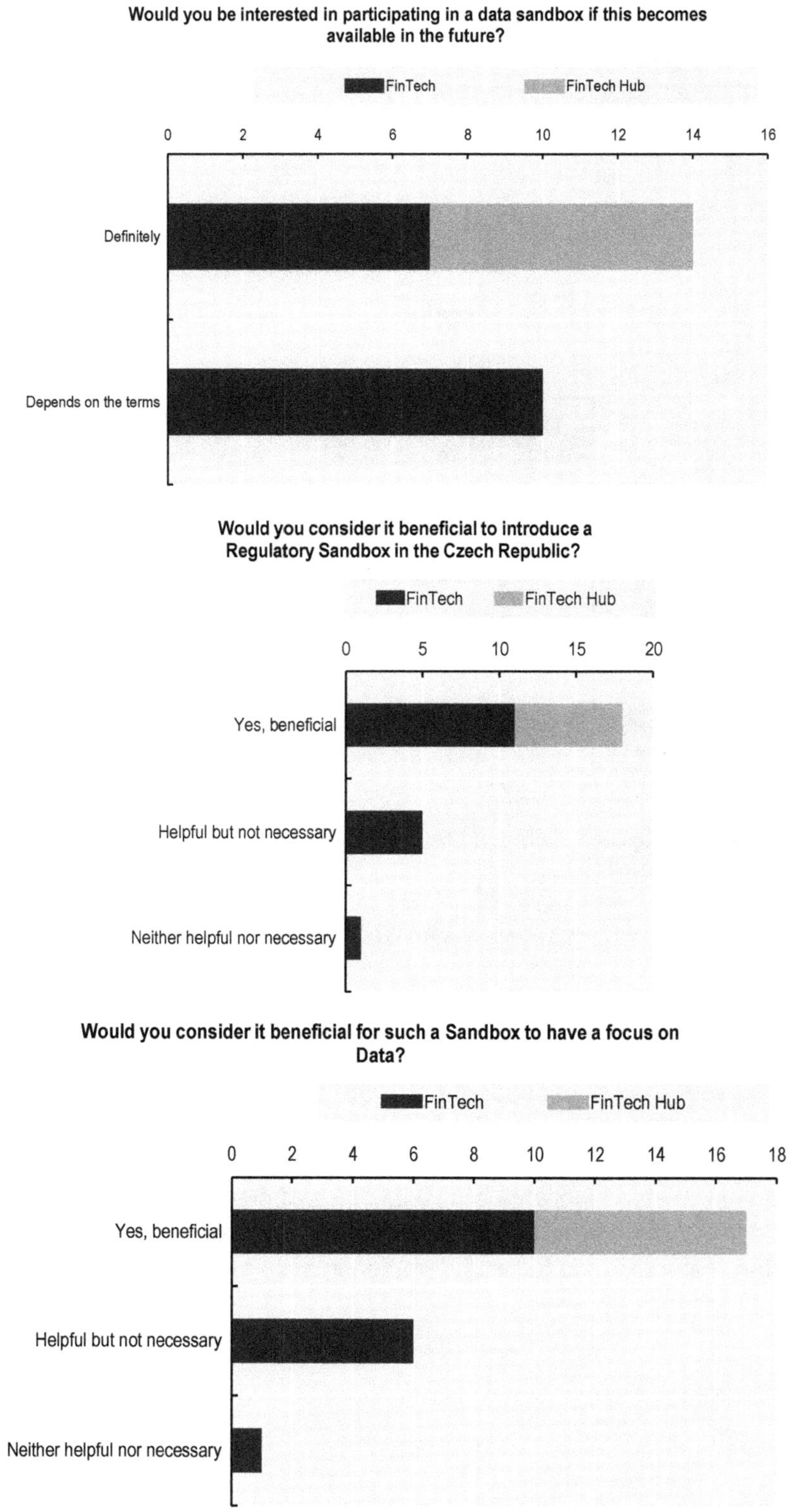

Source: Based on a sample of 24 responses by Czech FinTechs to the OECD Questionnaire.

Sandbox arrangements enable firms to test innovative financial products and services and develop business models that are based on the use of innovative technologies and mechanisms, subject to the specific rules applied by the supervisory authorities. Although sandboxes can involve the use of legally provided discretions by supervisory authorities, the baseline assumption for regulatory sandboxes is that firms are required to comply with all relevant rules applicable to the activity they are undertaking (BIS, 2018[19]). In addition, sandboxes do not entail the disapplication of regulatory requirements that must be applied as a result of EU law (ESMA, EBA and EIOPA, 2018[20]; Parenti, 2020[21]).

Regulatory sandboxes can foster innovation in the financial sector while allowing supervisors to observe and address emerging risks of the deployment of innovative technologies in finance, with benefits that extend to all stakeholders involved. They allow supervisors to enhance their understanding of innovative mechanisms deployed by FinTechs that may alter the risk profile of certain financial activities, which, in turn, may have a beneficial impact on the development of adequate policy responses to such innovations. Importantly, they reduce regulatory uncertainty for FinTechs and can help lower the perceived regulatory burden that has been observed in the OECD survey of FinTechs in the Czech Republic. In terms of funding, empirical evidence suggests a beneficial impact of sandbox participation for fundraising of companies, facilitating access to finance which has been highlighted as one of the most important impediments to the establishment and growth of SMEs in the Czech Republic and beyond (Cornelli et al., 2020[22]). Sandboxes can also promote competition, and allow for the development of new products and services, diversifying financial consumer offering and possibly promoting financial inclusion or other policy objectives, such as sustainability (FCA, 2022[23]).

When it comes to a data sandbox, this could conceptually involve a controlled environment on which FinTechs could test innovations on the basis of data sharing, data usage and business models that rely heavily on data. For example, the development, testing and validation of artificial intelligence-based products and of machine-learning-based models could be envisaged in a controlled environment of a data sandbox, or distributed ledger technology-based activity could be developed for the recording and analysis of large volumes of (unstructured) data. Indicatively, such data sandbox could provide real and synthetic datasets available through the sandbox or collected through API calls or could consist of an effort to collectively gather such datasets in co-operation with participating firms and depending on their needs.

4.6. Other important findings

Other noteworthy findings of the OECD Questionnaire suggest that the FinTech sector is largely male-dominated in the Czech Republic based on the survey sample. Although women are half of the country's population, less than 25% of FinTech employees are females (Figure 4.13). The proportion of female ICT specialists is the second lowest in the EU after Hungary (EU 2022).

Bringing in more women could increase the productivity of firms and could also widen the set of possible solutions and innovations. One of the potentials of FinTechs is to bring financial services to underserved populations, and female customers are one of them (IDB, 2022[24]; CCAF, 2021[25]; Chen et al., 2021[26]; Loko and Yang, 2022[27]).

Figure 4.13. Percentage of female employees in the FinTech sector

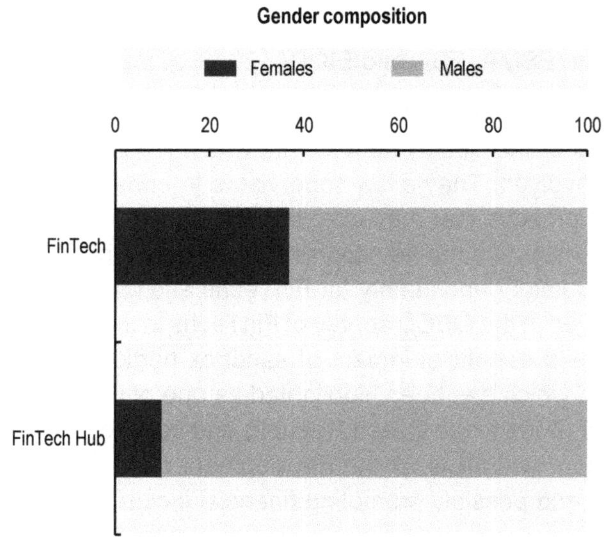

Source: Based on a sample of 24 responses by Czech FinTechs to the OECD Questionnaire.

In terms of expected impact of forthcoming regulations, PSD2 appears to have the most impact on FinTechs responding to the OECD survey, with AML also scoring high. This is very much consistent with the heavy reliance of the business models concerned on data and APIs, discussed above.

Figure 4.14. Czech FinTech perception of regulation, 2022

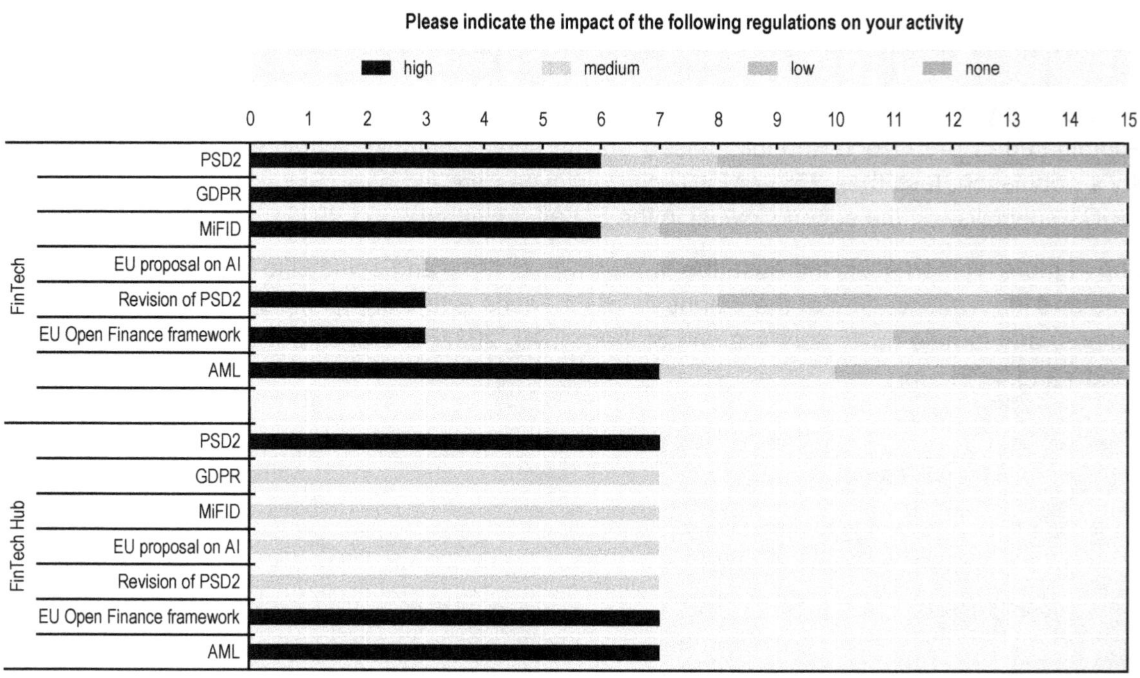

Source: Based on a sample of 24 responses by Czech FinTechs to the OECD Questionnaire.

Box 4.1. Survey "Start-ups and state" by Czech founders

In June 2022, Czech founders, an informal and non-profit platform of Czech start-up founders, published the results of a "Start-ups and state" survey performed in co-operation with Deloitte and the Confederation of Industry and Transport. The survey was based on responses by 156 company representatives and provides a perspective of the start-up situation in the Czech Republic.

According to the survey, there are three main obstacles in the Czech Republic identified by Czech start-ups: inadequate legal framework for employee share and stock option plans; hiring conditions for employees, including foreigners; and the need for a simplification of tax bureaucracy. Other problematic issues noted in the survey were what was noted as an unclear tax system, high employee costs and regulation of cryptocurrencies, particularly the possibility of financing through ICOs.

The survey also called for greater availability of grants for new jobs, as current grants set out conditions that are perceived as very difficult to be met by start-ups that are they are mostly operating in deficit in their first years of operation.

Importantly, one of the topics touched upon in the survey was the availability of public data for innovative product development, which 52% of respondents being dissatisfied. Another 66% of respondents further stating that they would like to use more public data or other sources for the development and testing of innovative products and services (including banking data for FinTech, open data for mobility, etc.)

Source: Czech Founders (2022[28]), Startupy a Stát, https://www.slideshare.net/VitHorky/startupy-a-stt-report-czech-founderspdf?from_action=save.

References

Berger, A. and G. Udell (2003), *Small Business and Debt Finance*, Springer-Verlag, https://doi.org/10.1007/0-387-24519-7_13. [16]

BIS (2018), "Implications of fintech developments for banks and bank supervisors", *Basel Committee on Banking Supervision, Sound Practices*, http://www.bis.org (accessed on 29 August 2022). [19]

Bromberg, L., A. Godwin and I. Ramsay (2017), "Fintech sandboxes: Achieving a balance between regulation and innovation", *Journal of Banking and Finance aw and Practice*, Vol. 28/4, pp. 314-336, https://papers.ssrn.com/sol3/papers.cfm?abstract_id=3090844 (accessed on 19 April 2022). [12]

CCAF (2021), *The 2nd Global Alternative Finance Market Benchmarking Report*, CCAF, https://www.jbs.cam.ac.uk/faculty-research/centres/alternative-finance/publications/the-2nd-global-alternative-finance-market-benchmarking-report/ (accessed on 25 January 2022). [25]

Chen, S. et al. (2021), "The fintech gender gap", BIS, https://www.bis.org/publ/work931.pdf (accessed on 11 October 2022). [26]

Citibank (2022), *Digital Money Index*, https://www.citibank.com/icg/sa/digital_symposium/digital_money_index/ (accessed on 29 August 2022). [6]

Cornelli, G. et al. (2020), "Inside the regulatory sandbox: effects on fintech funding", BIS, https://www.bis.org/publ/work901.htm (accessed on 29 August 2022). [22]

Czech Founders (2022), *Startupy a Stát*, https://www.slideshare.net/VitHorky/startupy-a-stt-report-czech-founderspdf?from_action=save (accessed on 4 August 2022). [28]

Deloitte Česká Republika (2022), *Jak se v Česku daří startupům*, https://www2.deloitte.com/cz/cs/pages/press/articles/jak-se-v-cesku-dari-startupum.html (accessed on 29 August 2022). [17]

ESMA, EBA and EIOPA (2018), *FinTech: Regulatory sandboxes and innovation hubs*, https://www.esma.europa.eu/sites/default/files/library/jc_2018_74_joint_report_on_regulatory_sandboxes_and_innovation_hubs.pdf (accessed on 29 August 2022). [20]

European Commission (2022), *Country Report-Czechia Accompanying the document Recommendation for a COUNCIL RECOMMENDATION on the 2022 National Reform Programme of Czechia and delivering a Council opinion on the 2022 Convergence Programme of Czechia*, https://eur-lex.europa.eu/legal-content/EN/ALL/?uri=CELEX%3A52022SC0605 (accessed on 29 August 2022). [14]

European Commission (2020), *Recommendation for a COUNCIL RECOMMENDATION on the 2020 National Reform Programme of Czechia and delivering a Council opinion on the 2020 Convergence Programme of Czechia*, https://eur-lex.europa.eu/legal-content/EN/TXT/?qid=1591720698631&uri=CELEX%3A52020DC0503 (accessed on 22 August 2022). [7]

European Commission (2019), *2019 European Semester: Assessment of progress on structural reforms, prevention and correction of macroeconomic imbalances, and results of in-depth reviews under Regulation (EU) No 1176/2011*, https://ec.europa.eu/info/sites/default/files/file_import/2019-european-semester-country-report-czech-republic_en.pdf (accessed on 11 October 2022). [15]

FCA (2022), *Supporting innovation in ESG data and disclosures: the digital sandbox sustainability pilot*, https://www.fca.org.uk/publication/corporate/digital-sandbox-sustainability-pilot-report.pdf (accessed on 22 August 2022). [23]

IDB (2022), *Fintech in Latin America and the Caribbean: A Consolidated Ecosystem for Recovery*, https://publications.iadb.org/en/fintech-latin-america-and-caribbean-consolidated-ecosystem-recovery (accessed on 23 August 2022). [24]

Kalifa, R. (2021), *Kalifa Review of UK Fintech*. [13]

Keogh, D. and D. Johnson (2021), "Survival of the funded: Econometric analysis of startup longevity and success", *Journal of Entrepreneurship, Management and Innovation*, Vol. 17/4, pp. 29-49, https://doi.org/10.7341/20211742. [18]

Loko, M. and Y. Yang (2022), "Fintech, Female Employment, and Gender Inequality", IMF, https://www.elibrary.imf.org/downloadpdf/journals/001/2022/108/001.2022.issue-108-en.pdf (accessed on 11 October 2022). [27]

Mnuchin, S. and C. Phillips (2018), *A Financial System That Creates Economic Opportunities Nonbank Financials, Fintech, and Innovation Report to President Donald J. Trump Executive Order 13772 on Core Principles for Regulating the United States Financial System Counselor to the Secretary*, US Department of Treasury, https://home.treasury.gov/sites/default/files/2018-08/A-Financial-System-that-Creates-Economic-Opportunities---Nonbank-Financials-Fintech-and-Innovation.pdf (accessed on 23 August 2022). [3]

Nassr, I. and G. Wehinger (2015), "Unlocking SME finance through market-based debt: Securitisation, private placements and bonds", *OECD Journal: Financial Market Trends* , Vol. 2014/2, https://www.oecd.org/finance/Unlocking-SME-finance-through-market-based-debt.pdf (accessed on 22 August 2022). [9]

OECD (2021), "Artificial Intelligence, Machine Learning and Big Data in Finance: Opportunities, Challenges, and Implications for Policy Makers", https://www.oecd.org/finance/financial-markets/Artificial-intelligence-machine-learning-big-data-in-finance.pdf (accessed on 11 October 2022). [2]

OECD (2020), *OECD Economic Surveys: Czech Republic 2020*, OECD Publishing, Paris, https://doi.org/10.1787/1b180a5a-en. [4]

OECD (2015), *Opportunities and Constraints of Market-Based Financing for SMEs OECD Report to G20 Finance Ministers and Central Bank Governors*, https://doi.org/10.1787/fmt-2014-5js3bg1g53ln. [8]

Parenti, R. (2020), "Regulatory sandboxes and innovation hubs for FinTech", *Study for the committee on Economic and Monetary Affairs, Policy Department for Economic, Scientific and Quality of Life Policies, European Parliament, Luxembourg,* September. [21]

World Bank (2022), *Regulation and Supervision of Fintech: Considerations for EMDE Policymakers*, https://openknowledge.worldbank.org/handle/10986/37345 (accessed on 23 August 2022). [1]

World Bank (2020), *Doing Business 2020*, https://doi.org/10.1596/978-1-4648-1440-2. [5]

World Bank (2020), "Global Experiences from Regulatory Sandboxes", *Fintech Note*, No. 8, World Bank, Washington DC, https://doi.org/10.1596/34789. [11]

World Bank (2020), "How Regulators Respond To FinTech : Evaluating the Different Approaches – Sandboxes and Beyond", *Fintech Note*, No. 4, https://doi.org/10.1596/33698. [10]

Annex A. Structure of the Czech financial ecosystem

This Annex describes the main stakeholders in the Czech financial ecosystem, which is composed of traditional incumbent financial intermediaries (banks, insurance companies, pension funds and investment funds) and BigTechs. A description of the local financial infrastructure including the payment system and capital markets is also included.

A rapid digitalisation trend in financial services, customer demands for a faster and more efficient delivery of financial products and services, as well as the recent COVID-19 pandemic have accelerated the global trend of fast-paced development of FinTech activity, including in the Czech market. Apart from FinTechs, platform-oriented firms, which are intrinsically technological and data-oriented, also have started providing payments and credit services, usually under the umbrella of accelerator labs focusing mostly in the payment services area. From the demand-side, both retail consumers and SMEs have contributed to increasing demand for digital financial services.

Figure A A.1. The Czech ecosystem for financial intermediation

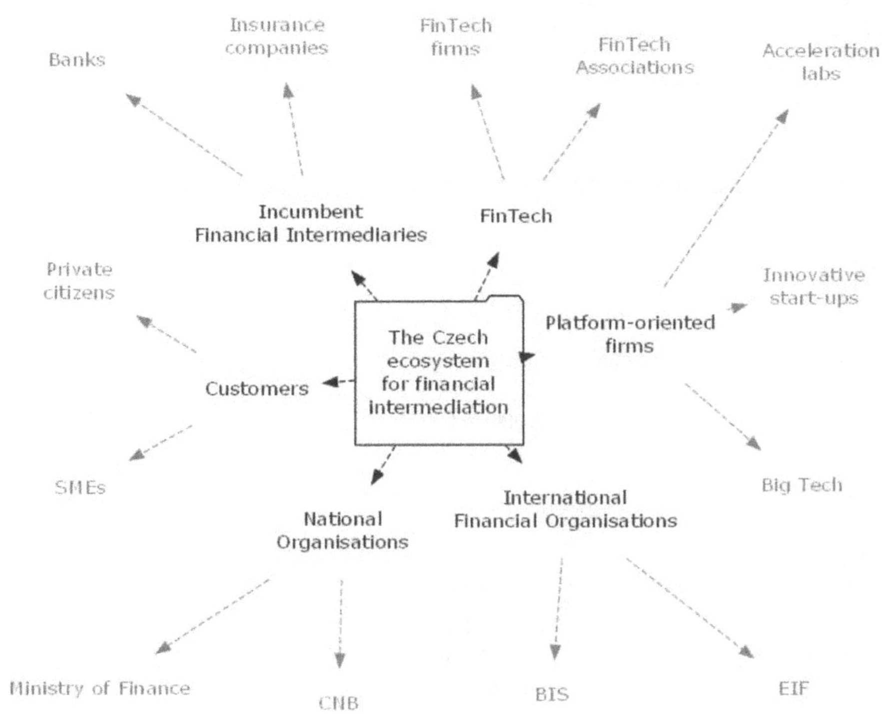

Figure A A.2. Czech regulated financial institutions

According to CNB classification

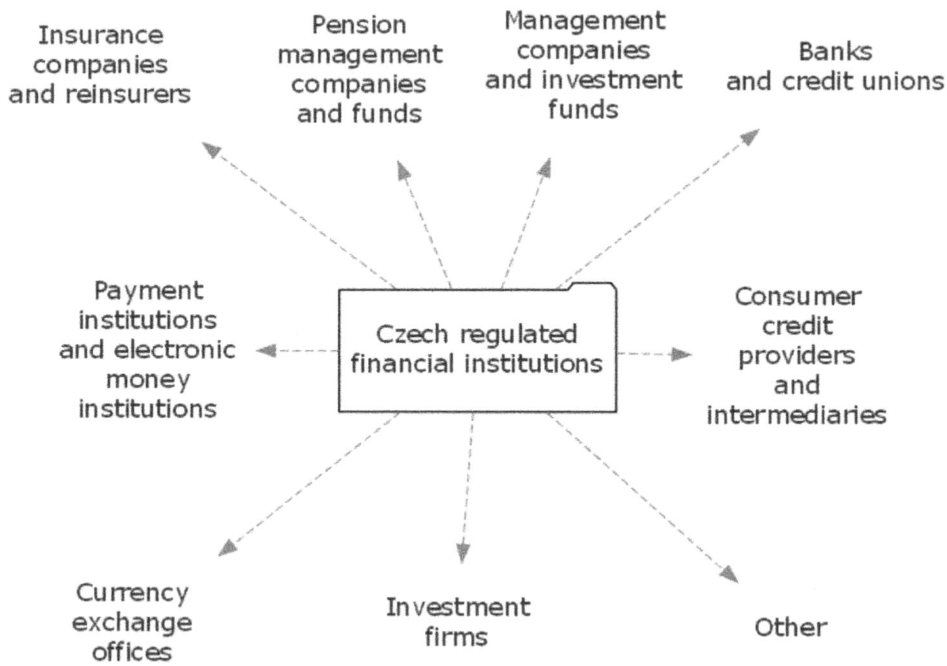

Source: CNB (2022[1]), Regulated institutions and registered financial market entities lists, https://apl.cnb.cz/apljerrsdad/JERRS.WEB07.INTRO_PAGE?p_lang=en.

Banks

The Czech financial system is largely dominated by banks, accounting for almost the totality of financial sector assets (Table A A.1).

Table A A.1. Czech Financial Sector Assets Distribution

As of 31 December 2021, in percentage of GDP

Sector	Assets (in CZK m)	% GDP
Banks	9, 469, 767	155.1%
Funds operated by pension management companies	577 951	9.5%
Insurance companies	518 202	8.5%
Investment funds	505 364	8.3%
Investment firms	33 158	0.5%
Pension management companies	15 189	0.2%
Credit unions	9 152	0.1%

Source: ARAD time series database of the CNB and the Czech Statistical Office.

The banking sector is rather concentrated, with the largest four banks accounting for almost two-thirds of assets (as of 31 March 2022, (CNB, 2022[2])). Foreign banks have established branches in the Czech Republic (22 foreign bank branches as of 31 December 2021, Table A A.2, Figure A A.3).

Table A A.2. Distribution of Czech banks, by size and ownership

As of 31 December 2021

Total number of banks	44
- Large banks (assets of over 10% of the total banking sector's assets)	4
- Medium-sized banks (assets between 2% and 10% of the total banking sector's assets)	5
- Small banks (assets less than 2% of the total banking sector's assets)	8
- Foreign bank branches	22
- Building societies	5
Czech-controlled banks	11
- of which are state-owned banks	2
Foreign-controlled bank	33

Source: ARAD time series database of the CNB.

Figure A A.3. Concentration in the Czech Banking Sector

In percentage, as of 31 December 2021

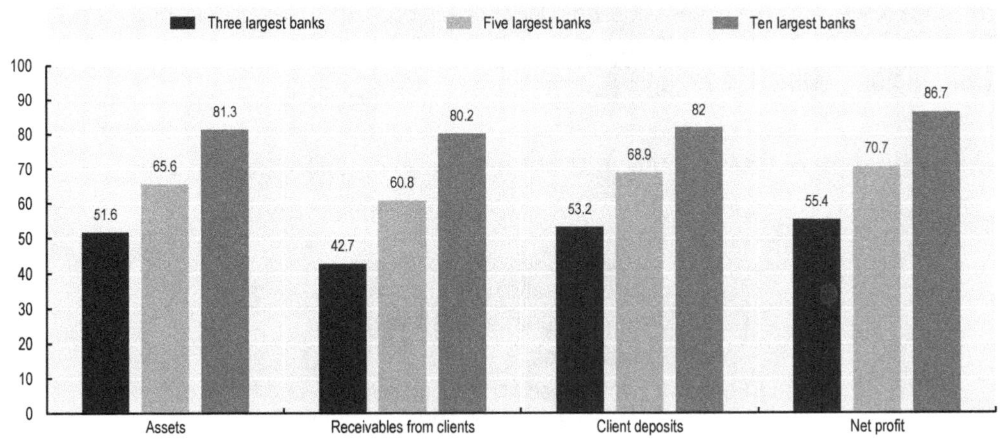

Source: CNB (2022[3]) Financial Market Supervision Report 2021 (in Czech), www.cnb.cz.

The Czech banking sector is well-capitalised and increasingly profitable. The total capital ratio, as a key factor in the sector's resilience, remained close to its long-term high of 23.5% in 2021. Pre-tax profit grew by almost 50% to EUR 3.46 bn (CZK 85.9 bn), up by EUR 1.14 bn (CZK 28.4 bn) year-on-year,[1] and is thus significantly closer to the levels achieved before the COVID-19 pandemic, mainly due to a decline in impairment losses in the context of a renewed decline in the share of non-performing loans. The Czech banking sector is almost 50% more profitable than the average EU banking sector, and such differential is especially notable when compared to Eurozone countries' banking sectors (MFCR, 2022[4]).

The possible drivers of bank dominance in the Czech Republic are public trust; customer loyalty and overall client satisfaction. Customers are used to choose primarily banks to satisfy all of their financial needs. Customer satisfaction in also high in terms of diversity of services offered by banks, with 66% of Czechs reporting that the banking system can satisfy all of their financial needs. There is also quite high level of trust in the banking system among Czech citizens, especially among university students, tradesmen, and in particular among residents of the capital city, Prague (MFCR, 2020[5]).

Ownership of banking sector

The Czech banking system is dominated by foreign-owned banks. Only about one-third of Czech banks is Czech owned (Table A A.2). All top three of the largest Czech banks (ČSOB, Česká spořitelna and Komerční banka) are foreign-owned (Olga Skalková, 2022[6]; Jana Divinová, 2022[7]).[2] There are two state-owned banks (Czech Export Bank and the Czech-Moravian Guarantee and Development Bank). 22 foreign bank branches are active in the Czech banking market as of 31 December 2021. Border services in the Czech Republic can also be provided by around 450 foreign banks operating in the EU's single internal market. Furthermore, there are two multination institutions active in the Czech market – European Investment Bank and European Bank for Reconstruction and Development. Czech banks co-operate with them and use their products such as loans and guarantees within the framework of InvestEU.

Insurance companies

There are 41 insurance companies operating on the Czech financial market (as of March 2022, (CNB, 2022[2])). The majority of them focus their activities in the non-life insurance sector and most of them are either owned by foreign entities or constitute branches of foreign-owned institutions (Table A A.3). The insurance sector has been growing steadily over the last five years, with the highest growth in the non-life segment, while life insurance continued its downward trend. The total number of insurance contracts in the Czech Republic was 30.4 m and the aggregate amount of premiums from all clients in 2021 was EUR 7.22 bn (CZK 179.6 bn) [EUR 2.08 bn (CZK 51.7 bn) in life insurance and EUR 5.14 bn (CZK 127.9 bn) in non-life insurance). The balance sheet total of the insurance sector was EUR 21.17 bn (CZK 526.2 bn) in 2021 (MFCR, 2022[4]).[3]

Table A A.3. Distribution of Czech insurance companies, by ownership and type

As of 31 March 2022

Total number of insurance firms	41
Czech-controlled insurance undertakings	12
- of which state-owned	1
Foreign-controlled insurance undertakings	11
Branches of foreign insurance undertakings	18
Life insurance undertakings	5
Non-life insurance undertaking	25
Composite insurance undertakings	11

Source: ARAD time series database of the CNB.

Pension funds

The first pillar of the pension system in the Czech Republic is the mandatory, defined-benefit, funded on a running basis ('Pay As You Go') public pension scheme. The system is universal and provides for all economically active individuals. It consists of an earnings-related component and a basic, flat-rate component. A second voluntary pillar, which is common in EU, meant for retirement savings, and based on employee-employer contributions was introduced in 2013, but shortly discontinued three years later (OECD, 2020[8]).

The third pillar, consisting of voluntary funded pension arrangements has been in place since 1994 and tough it covers 52% of the working age population, the assets under management for this part represent only 9% of GDP as of 2020 (OECD, 2020[8]). There are currently 4.44 million persons participating in the third pillar and the total volume of participants' funds is EUR 22.8 bn (CZK 566.7 bn) (MFCR, 2022[4]).[4,5] These savings are managed by private pension companies. Until 2013, the supplementary pension insurance scheme required pension funds to guarantee a non-negative return on annual basis, which was cancelled thereafter. The legacy funds are now called transformed funds. The Czech market of pension management companies is moderately concentrated; as of March 2022 there were only nine pension management companies in the Czech market (CNB, 2022[2]). At the end of 2019, the pension management companies were managing assets in 36 pension funds, of which 28 participating funds and eight transformed funds. In addition, the two largest companies managed 45% of the assets for 46% of the participants (OECD, 2020[8]).

Competition level among pension managers does not seem to be strong; pension management companies usually charge the maximum allowed by law with few exceptions, switches are uncommon, pension management companies have increasing profits due to higher fee income. Three of the pension management companies are subsidiaries of banks and use the banks' network for the distribution of their funds (OECD, 2020[8]).

Investment returns on funded schemes have been mostly declining in the Czech Republic over the years, both in nominal and real terms due to conservative investment strategy; in international comparison, the Czech Republic is among the OECD countries with the lowest average performance over the 5-15 years ending in 2018. The young age of the contributory system, low contribution levels and low performance all contribute to the overall low ranking of the Czech Republic complementary pension system in terms of assets under management to GDP among the OECD (OECD, 2020[8]).

On average in OECD countries, people older than 65 have a disposable income equal to 87% of the total population; The Czech Republic is well below that with 74%, with old-age pension being the most important component of old-age income (OECD, 2020[8]).

Investment funds

Compared to 2020, the volume of assets under management in investment funds increased significantly to EUR 35.78 bn (CZK 889.5 bn),[6] although it still remains a very small part of total [financial assets] in the system. The recent increase may be driven by the growth in asset prices on global markets over the year 2021 and the increase in investment inflows by clients (MFCR, 2022[4]).

In the Czech Republic, there are ordinary collective investment funds, in which anyone can invest, and qualified investor funds, in which investors must meet specific conditions. Collective investment funds can be set up in two forms, either as mutual funds in which the unitholder owns a unit certificate or as a joint stock company that collects funds from the public by issuing shares and then invests them, based on a risk-spreading investment strategy. The essence of collective investment is the pooling of funds from individual 'retail' investors. Collective investment funds dominate the sector and the volume of funds in collective investment funds increased by 20% year-on-year to an all-time high of EUR 28.46 bn (CZK 707.6 bn) in 2021, of which EUR 17.69 bn (CZK 439.7 bn) (62.1%) were domestic funds and EUR 10.77 bn (CZK 267.9 bn) (37.9%) were foreign funds[7] (MFCR, 2022[4]).

Only qualified investors who meet one of two requirements may invest in the qualified investor fund. These requirements are to either invest at least EUR 125 000 in the fund and at the same time declare that the investor has sufficient knowledge of the investment instruments used by the fund and understands all the risks involved, or by making an investment exceeding EUR 40 225.26 (CZK 1 000 000) if the investor proves to the fund administrator that the investment is appropriate to his/her financial background, investment objectives and professional knowledge and experience. These funds then have, for example, looser investment limits compared to collective investment funds or allow investment in a wider range of investment instruments. Qualified investor funds are also subdivided into open-end and closed-end funds, which represent a narrower group of investors and do not accept new deposits. The volume of money under management in a Qualified Investor Fund increased by almost a quarter year-on-year to EUR 7.3 bn (CZK 181.9 bn)[8] in 2021, which amounts to about one-fifth of the assets under management of the entire investment sector (MFCR, 2022[4]).

Payments

This section describes the infrastructure of the payment systems in the Czech Republic: this comprises the settlement system – the Czech Express Real-Time Interbank Gross Settlement system CERTIS, instant payments and payments per contact.

CERTIS

The CERTIS is a payment system operated by the CNB through which the Czech domestic payments are intermediated. This excludes cases where the payer's and payee's accounts are held within the same bank, in which case the payment is settled within the bank's own system. CERTIS does not provide interbank payments in foreign currency. For this purpose, banks use foreign payment settlement systems or correspondent banking mechanisms. The CNB maintains the accounts for banks, branches of foreign banks, savings and credit co-operatives, which are the only financial institutions allowed to participate directly in CERTIS. Other non-bank providers of payment services are not allowed to participate in CERTIS[9] (CNB, 2022[9]).

Instant payments

Instant payments were introduced to the Czech financial market in 2019 and have been widely used since then. The instant payments infrastructure is operated by the CNB via the CERTIS system, and the services are provided to customers by banks who have voluntarily joined the service. Instant payments enable customer to transfer Czech Crowns at any time and the median processing time between the time at which the payer's bank sends an instruction to CERTIS to execute the payment and the time at which the payee's bank receives the instant payment from CERTIS is 0.5 seconds (CNB, 2022[10]). As of 1 January 2022, this service was provided by 13 Czech banks and one-in-five transactions is currently performed in instant payment mode.

Payment per contact

The most recent initiative which will be provided by the CNB is the so-called Payments per Contact. It will allow payments to be executed based on the phone number of the recipient instead of the corresponding bank account number. That service will be possible due to the pairing of the register of account numbers with the mobile numbers of their owners. After the payment has been made, the sender's bank will obtain the recipient's bank account from the contact registry and send the payment.

The CNB is currently working on this project with the Czech banking Association and started the testing of this project during the summer of 2022. In the meantime, nine banks have so far signed up for offering this service, however, if the customer wants to receive payments through this method, they must specifically sign up for it through their bank and link their phone number to their account number. The full implementation of the payments per contract is expected in 2023 (CNB, 2022[11]).

BigTechs and other platform-based companies

BigTech increasingly leverage their free access to vast amounts of customer data that feed into AI-driven models to provide financial services across OECD and non-OECD economies. Practically all banks in the Czech Republic also offer Google Pay or Apple Pay.[10] In fact, according to industry sources, almost 25% of all card payments in the Czech Republic are intermediated through Apple or Google Pay (Mobil Mania, 2022[12])

The use of customer data by BigTech raises risks around data privacy and concerns over ways in which the collection, storage and use of personal data that are exploited for commercial gain. Access to customer data by BigTech gives them a clear competitive advantage over smaller FinTech and start-ups, and possible even over conventional financial services providers. This advantage is likely to be further reinforced with their use of AI, which offers possibilities for novel, customised and more efficient service provision by these players. The dominance of BigTech in certain areas of the market could lead to excessive market concentration and increase the dependence of the market to few large BigTech players, with possible systemic implications depending on their scale and scope (OECD, 2021[13]). It should be highlighted that BigTech can use their data advantage to build monopolistic positions, both in relation to client acquisition (for example through effective price discrimination) and through the introduction of high barriers to entry for smaller players. Another related risk has to do with anti-competitive behaviours and market concentration in the technology aspect of the service provision (e.g. cloud services).

Capital markets

The government of the Czech Republic has concluded that the capital market in the Czech Republic is underdeveloped and not sufficiently fulfilling its main function (i.e. to efficiently redistribute free financial resources from savers and investors (households) to entrepreneurs who need to finance their development). One of the likely reasons for that is that traditional bank financing such as deposits or loans prevails, while there is also a strong reliance on EU subsidies (but not necessarily in the FinTech sector) (MFCR, 2019[14]). This bias toward bank finance is supported by conservative asset allocation of households (Figure A A.4) low savings for old age on top of the mandatory pension provisions, low awareness among entrepreneurs of the possibilities of financing business and research through the capital market, and a small range of domestic investment instruments available to retail investors compared to Western Europe. Due to the fact that exchange-traded stocks and bonds do not play a significant role in corporate financing in the Czech Republic, small and medium-sized enterprises in particular are heavily dependent on financing through retained earnings and bank loans (MFCR, 2019[15]).

Figure A A.4. Currency and Deposits held by Households, 2020

Percentage of total financial assets

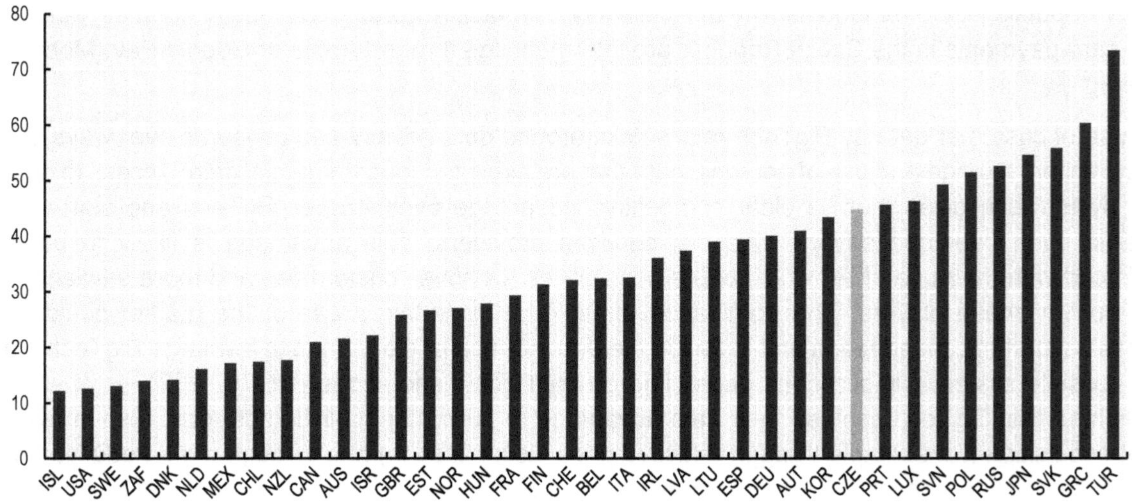

Source: OECD, Household financial assets (indicator).

Even though the Czech capital market is not as big and liquid as the markets of the countries that joined the EU before 2004, it ranks among the best compared to countries that joined EU in 2004 (both in terms of market cap to GDP adjusted for population size and in terms of trading volume). However, an observed decline in liquidity in recent years may jeopardise the interest of investors and issuers (MFCR, 2019[15]).

To tackle the issue of underdeveloped capital markets, the MFCR has prepared a Capital Market Development Conception (2019-30) which was approved by the government and apart from analysing the current state of the Czech financial market, it suggest four main actions (each targeted at a different group of stakeholders – households, businesses, market infrastructure and the public sector) (MFCR, 2019[15]). A progress report will be submitted on 31 December 2022, in particular with regard to some of the specific indicators monitored such as the market capitalisation of the Prague Stock Exchange and trading volumes on it, the way Czech businesses are financed and the composition of savings of Czech households in order to see the successfulness of the actions. The official roles of the MFCR in the field of capital market are to develop financial market policies, carry out its analysis, draft capital market laws, be a mandatory point of comment on legislation relating to the capital market area, and ensure a membership in international financial institutions and European Union bodies as regards the capital market area. The ministry has also launched an informational website called Capital Guide which is intended for SMEs looking for alternatives to bank financing for their business. On this website they can, for example, find out which financing instrument is best suited to their situation, find a relevant legal or financial advisor that can help with the process or experiences of other businesses that have been in the same position (MFCR and EU, 2022[16]).

The Structure of the local capital market

There are three trading platforms in the Czech Republic – Prague Stock Exchange, RM-SYSTÉM and the Czech Stock Exchange, two settlement system operators with the irrevocability of settlement (Central Securities Depository and the Czech National Bank as the operator of the Short-Term Bond System), one Central Depository (Central Securities Depository) and one administrator of benchmarks, namely the Prague Interbank Offered Rate – PRIBOR (Czech Financial Benchmark Facility).

Stock market

The largest stock exchange is the Prague Stock Exchange (PSE) which is a subsidiary of Wiener Börse and uses the same trading platform. It also fully meets the EU standards (such as trading hours or disclosure requirements, quarterly reporting etc.). There are 16 share issues on the Prime Market and Standard Market, nine share issues on the START market, 29 share issues on the Free Market, 32 issues of collective investment securities, 123 issues of bonds and stripped coupons 107 issues of investment certificates and warrants admitted to trading on the exchange at the end of 2021.[11]

PSE currently operates three venues in which companies' shares are offered and traded. These are primarily the STANDARD and PRIME markets, while there is also the smaller START market intended for SMEs. To make it easier, faster, with lower cost, and in general more accessible for the companies to publicly offer their stocks, The Prague Stock Exchange came up with a special trading venue targeted at smaller, usually innovative companies with a minimum capitalisation of EUR 1.02 m (CZK 25 m) to maximum capitalisation of EUR 82 m (CZK 2 bn)[12] which are looking to raise new capital. The venue is called START market and it might be also useful for business owners who want to fully or partially exit from the company (Prague Stock Exchange, 2022[17]). If the company wants to enter the START market is must meet the following conditions: registered as a joint-stock company (a. s.) or as a European company (SE), registered seat in the Czech Republic, audit covering most recent two or three years, or the entirety of the company's existence, use Czech accounting standards, offer a large enough shareholding to create sufficient liquidity [ideally between EUR 1.02 m and 2.04 m (CZK 25 m and 50 m) [13]] (MFCR and EU, 2022[18]). The process is then more affordable and faster because the issuer can submit only a simplified version of a prospectus. However, even though the requirements are lower (less costly/fewer requirements/require lower market cap?) than for the standard markets, the companies in START market still have flexible options for raising capital in future rounds. PSE also organises twice a year the so-called START Days during which market issuers, investors and representatives of companies that are planning to enter the START market meet a discuss business results or plans (MFCR and EU, 2022[18]).

Apart from the START market, two other markets are offered by the Prague Stock Exchange. The STANDARD Market and the PRIME Market which are both intended for the trading of shares of large Czech and foreign companies and the issuers must meet either the more stringent conditions of the official securities market or the statutory requirements governing the regulated market. PSE also permits the listing of shares without the consent of the issuer if they are already traded on another regulated market within the EU. To trade on the STANDARD and PRIME markets, the issuers must have a market capitalisation of issue no less than EUR 1 m (CZK 24.4 m),[14] free float (a portion of issue in the hands of public investors) of at least 25% and it must exist for at least three years (MFCR and EU, 2022[18]). The time to complete an IPO usually takes from six to nine months, the first Special purpose acquisition companies (SPAC) are therefore starting to emerge in the Czech financial market because through SPAC companies can enter the stock market only in about two months (Jiří Zatloukal, 2022[19]).

Bond markets

To issue a bond without a prospectus in a public offering, which might be especially useful for small and medium enterprises, is possible if the value of the offer does not exceed EUR 1 m [or an equivalent in Czech Crown (CZK 24.4 million)[15] over a period of 12 months]. This possibility significantly reduces the bond placements costs. These offerings are typically worth between EUR 410 000 and EUR 820 000 (CZK 10 m and CZK 20 m).[16] Bond issues above the abovementioned threshold cannot be issued to the public without publishing a prospectus. Alternatively, a private offering to accredited investors, or to no more than 149 natural persons, can be used. The law also limits the maximum volume of financial resources to be raised through the issuing of bonds to retail investors. When issuing bonds with a prospectus in cases where the offerings exceed EUR 1 m (CZK 24.4 m)[17] in value, the prospectus must contain information about the terms of the issue, the sale and repayment of the bonds, the financial status of the issuer and the identification of potential risks of failure to repay the bonds issued (MFCR and EU, 2022[20]).

Table A A.4. Estimated costs of bond placement

Cost entry	Issue w/o prospectus	Issue w/o prospectus	Issue with prospectus
Issue size	CZK 100 m	CZK 150 m	CZK 300 m
Legal counsel	CZK 100 000 – 150 000	CZK 100 000 – 150 000	CZK 200 000 – 300 000
Fixed costs of transactions	CZK 700 000 – 1m	CZK 700 000 – 1 m	CZK 700 000 – 1 m
Variable costs of transaction (3-5%)	CZK 3 m – 5 m	CZK 4.5 m – 7.5 m	CZK 6 m – 12 m
Additional counsel (optional)	-	-	-
Total one-off costs	CZK 3.8 m – 6.15 m	CZK 5.3 m – 8.65 m	CZK 6.9 m – 13.3 m
Total one-off costs as %	3.80 – 6.15%	3.50 – 5.77%	2.30 – 4.43%
Annual administration cost	CZK 200 000 –400 000	CZK 300 000 – 600 000	CZK 600 000 – 1.2 m

Source: MFCR and EU (2022[20]), Bond markets | Capital guide, https://www.kapitalovypruvodce.cz/en/dluhove-nastroje/trh-s-dluhopisy/.

References

CNB (2022), *ARAD - Time Serie System - Czech National bank*, https://www.cnb.cz/cnb/STAT.ARADY_PKG.STROM_DRILL?p_strid=0&p_lang=EN (accessed on 4 August 2022). [2]

CNB (2022), *CERTIS – the interbank payment system – description - Czech National Bank*, https://www.cnb.cz/en/payments/certis/certis-the-interbank-payment-system-description/ (accessed on 30 August 2022). [9]

CNB (2022), *Financial Market Supervision Report 2021 (in Czech)*, http://www.cnb.cz (accessed on 4 August 2022). [3]

CNB (2022), *Instant payments – description*, https://www.cnb.cz/en/payments/certis/instant-payments-description/ (accessed on 30 August 2022). [10]

CNB (2022), *K zaslání peněz už nebude nutné znát číslo účtu. Banky ve spolupráci s ČNB připravují tzv. platby na kontakt*, https://www.cnb.cz/cs/cnb-news/tiskove-zpravy/K-zaslani-penez-uz-nebude-nutne-znat-cislo-uctu.-Banky-ve-spolupraci-s-CNB-pripravuji-tzv.-platby-na-kontakt/ (accessed on 4 August 2022). [11]

CNB (2022), *Regulated institutions and registered financial market entities lists*, https://apl.cnb.cz/apljerrsdad/JERRS.WEB07.INTRO_PAGE?p_lang=en (accessed on 17 June 2022). [1]

Jana Divinová (2022), *Kdo vlastní banky v Česku a které jsou české. Přehled majitelů*, peníze.cz, https://www.penize.cz/osobni-ucty/429689-kdo-vlastni-banky-v-cesku-a-ktere-jsou-ceske-prehled-majitelu (accessed on 4 August 2022). [7]

Jiří Zatloukal (2022), "Poprvé v Česku. Na burzu vstupuje prázdná schránka a hledá další „Pilulku“", *Seznam Zprávy*, https://www.seznamzpravy.cz/clanek/ekonomika-finance-na-prazskou-burzu-vstupuje-prazdna-firma-a-hleda-dalsi-pilulku-187786 (accessed on 31 August 2022). [19]

MFCR (2022), *Report on Financial Market Developments in 2021 (in Czech)*, https://www.mfcr.cz/assets/cs/media/2022-06-30_Zprava-o-vyvoji-financniho-trhu-v-roce-2021_v02.pdf (accessed on 4 August 2022). [4]

MFCR (2020), *Financial Literacy Measurement Results 2020: ATTITUDES TO FINANCE AND BEHAVIOR ON THE FINANCIAL MARKET*, https://financnigramotnost.mfcr.cz/cs/pro-odborniky/mereni-urovne-financni-gramotnosti/2020/postoje-k-financim-a-chovani-3272/ (accessed on 4 August 2022). [5]

MFCR (2019), *National Strategy for the Development of the Capital Market in the Czech Republic for the period of 2019-2023*, https://www.mfcr.cz/assets/en/media/201903-National-Strategy-CZ-Capital-Market.pdf (accessed on 1 July 2022). [14]

MFCR (2019), *National Strategy for the Development of the Capital Market in the Czech Republic for the period of 2019-2023*, https://www.mfcr.cz/assets/en/media/201903-National-Strategy-CZ-Capital-Market.pdf (accessed on 1 July 2022). [15]

MFCR and EU (2022), *Bond markets | Capital guide*, https://www.kapitalovypruvodce.cz/en/dluhove-nastroje/trh-s-dluhopisy/ (accessed on 23 August 2022). [20]

MFCR and EU (2022), *Home | Capital guide*, https://www.kapitalovypruvodce.cz/en/ (accessed on 5 August 2022). [16]

MFCR and EU (2022), *Stock markets | Capital guide*, https://www.kapitalovypruvodce.cz/en/kapitalove-nastroje/akciove-trhy/ (accessed on 31 August 2022). [18]

Mobil Mania (2022), *Před 10 lety jsme v Česku začali platit mobilem. Start byl divoký, dnes tak „pípá" každý čtvrtý – MobilMania.cz*, https://mobilmania.zive.cz/clanky/pred-10-lety-jsme-v-cesku-zacali-platit-mobilem-start-byl-divoky-dnes-tak-pipa-kazdy-ctvrty/sc-3-a-1355850/default.aspx (accessed on 1 November 2022). [12]

OECD (2021), "Artificial Intelligence, Machine Learning and Big Data in Finance: Opportunities, Challenges, and Implications for Policy Makers", https://www.oecd.org/finance/financial-markets/Artificial-intelligence-machine-learning-big-data-in-finance.pdf (accessed on 11 October 2022). [13]

OECD (2020), *OECD Reviews of Pension Systems: Czech Republic*, OECD Reviews of Pension Systems, OECD Publishing, Paris, https://doi.org/10.1787/e6387738-en. [8]

Olga Skalková (2022), *Největší banky v Česku. Nové žebříčky podle klientů a peněz*, peníze.cz, https://www.penize.cz/osobni-ucty/432939-nejvetsi-banky-v-cesku-zebricek-podle-poctu-klientu-a-spravovanych-penez (accessed on 4 August 2022). [6]

Prague Stock Exchange (2022), *START Market*, https://www.pse.cz/en/trading/markets/start-market (accessed on 31 August 2022). [17]

Notes

[1] Based on exchange rate as of 31 December 2021 which was CZK 24.860 for EUR 1

[2] ČSOB by a Belgian company KBC Bank N.V., Česká spořitelna by an Austrian company Erste Group Bank AG and Komerční banka by a French company Société Générale S.A.

[3] Based on exchange rate as of 31 December 2021 which was CZK 24.860 for EUR 1

[4] The average monthly contribution of a participant was CZK 781 under the supplementary pension scheme and CZK 829 under the supplementary pension savings scheme in 2021 and the state support paid to the participants of the third pillar in the same year was CZK 7.6 bn. Employer can also contribute to the pension savings scheme.

[5] Based on exchange rate as of 31 December 2021 which was CZK 24.860 for EUR 1

[6] Based on exchange rate as of 31 December 2021 which was CZK 24.860 for EUR 1

[7] Based on exchange rate as of 31 December 2021 which was CZK 24.860 for EUR 1

[8] Based on exchange rate as of 31 December 2021 which was CZK 24.860 for EUR 1

[9] A group of so-called "third parties" are allowed to submit "third party orders" in CERTIS under a special status and a bilateral agreements with CNB. This category is distinct from TTPs, third-party payment providers, mentioned in Section 2.2.4. It refers to non-bank financial infrastructure type of institutions, for example card payment clearing houses and the securities clearing and settlement. They have no interbank payment account with the CNB but, with the permission of the direct participants concerned, can submit payment orders to CERTIS to transfer funds between direct participants (e.g. to settle the summarised positions arising from the card payment clearing or payments relating to stock exchange transactions).

[10] List of banks that offer Google Pay: https://pay.google.com/intl/cs_cz/about/banks/ and Apple pay: https://support.apple.com/cs-cz/HT206637

[11] Response from the Czech Banking Association to the OECD questionnaire

[12] Based on exchange rate as of 14 July 2022 which was CZK 24.4 for EUR 1

[13] Based on exchange rate as of 14 July 2022 which was CZK 24.4 for EUR 1

[14] Based on exchange rate as of 14 July 2022 which was CZK 24.4 for EUR 1

[15] Based on exchange rate as of 14 July 2022 which was CZK 24.4 for EUR 1

[16] Based on exchange rate as of 14 July 2022 which was CZK 24.4 for EUR 1

[17] Based on exchange rate as of 14 July 2022 which was CZK 24.4 for EUR 1

Annex B. Macro-prudential responsibilities and tools of the CNB

The CNB's mandate for conducting macroprudential policy is laid down in Act No. 6/1993 Coll., on the Czech National Bank, which stipulates that the CNB shall, among other things, maintain financial stability. The CNB is expressly entrusted to "identify, monitor and assess risks jeopardising the stability of the financial system and, in order to prevent or mitigate these risks, contribute by means of its powers to the resilience of the financial system and the maintenance of financial stability; where necessary, it must co-operate with the relevant state authorities in setting macroprudential policy". The unit at the CNB responsible for financial stability and macroprudential policy comes under the broader remit of financial market supervision. It therefore works in close co-operation with other CNB supervisory units responsible for safeguarding and maintaining the individual stability of financial market entities (CNB, 2020[1]).

The CNB's pursuit of macroprudential policy is based on powers laid down in the legislation in force in the Czech Republic – Above all, Articles 2e) and 2d) of Act No. 6/1993 Coll., on the CNB, 26 Article of Act No. 21/1992 Coll., on Banks, Directive No 2013/36/EU of the European Parliament and of the Council (CRD) and Regulation (EU) No 575/2013 of the European Parliament and of the Council (CRR) (CNB, 2020[1]).

The legal basis for CNB's macroprudential policy duties was amended into the Act on the CNB, e.g. the option of issuing recommendations, alerts or warnings to the public or to individuals, the general authority to impose remedial measures in the event of a breach of any sectoral regulation, and changes in the reporting and statistics framework. The amendment also forbids searches in inspection files and allows decisions to be changed (not only revoked) in appeals proceedings in all sectors (CNB, 2014[2]).

The CNB applies its macroprudential instruments both individually and simultaneously and has the following tool types at his disposal (CNB, 2020[1]):

- Legally binding instruments applied to entities regulated and supervised by the CNB, non-compliance with which is subject to penalties. Instruments defined in Czech law have the strongest legal position. They include: instruments relating to capital, capital buffers, risk weights of exposures, liquidity and concentration of assets, mostly those of the banking sector; and instruments which the CNB may use for a period of six months (in the form of a provision of a general nature) to mitigate the consequences of or to curb risks which are not anticipated and relate to the banking sector.
- Instruments based on recommendations, which are not laid down directly in the legislation. The CNB uses these instruments to recommend specific responses to regulated or other entities in order to reduce risks to financial stability. Recommendations may be public or confidential. They are legally unenforceable.
- Communication instruments.

The CNB has a set of macroprudential instruments that it applies mostly to the banking sector. Macroprudential policy also covers non-banking components of the financial system. The CNB assesses the activities and position of non-bank financial institutions on an ongoing basis and, where necessary, responds to changes in systemic risk and resilience. The CNB also sees a need for a debate about the medium-term systemic risks associated with pension management companies, management companies, pension funds and investment funds. In this area, the CNB supports better management of investment and liquidity risks by investment and pension management funds, management companies and pension management companies, transparency towards holders of fund units regarding risk perceptions, and, last but not least, financial and investment literacy of households (CNB, 2020[1]).

References

CNB (2020), *The CNB's Macroprudential Policy Strategy*, https://www.cnb.cz/export/sites/cnb/en/financial-stability/.galleries/macroprudential_policy/cnb_macroprudential_policy_strategy.pdf (accessed on 6 July 2022). [1]

CNB (2014), *Financial Market Supervision Report 2013*, https://www.cnb.cz/export/sites/cnb/en/supervision-financial-market/.galleries/aggregate_information_financial_sector/financial_market_supervision_reports/download/fms_2013.pdf (accessed on 6 July 2022). [2]

www.ingramcontent.com/pod-product-compliance
Lightning Source LLC
Chambersburg PA
CBHW061223240926
51846CB00006B/1332
* 9 7 8 9 2 6 4 6 3 5 7 3 9 *